# John Heyl Vincent's
# REMINISCENCES

John H. Vincent, 1888

*Courtesy of Bridwell Library Special Collections, SMU, Dallas, Texas.*

# John Heyl Vincent's REMINISCENCES

*Autobiographical Writings of the Founding Superintendent of Chautauqua*

EDITED BY TIMOTHY S. BINKLEY

BRIDWELL PRESS
Southern Methodist University
Dallas, Texas

Bridwell Press is the professional
publishing arm of Bridwell Library
(SMU Libraries and Perkins School of Theology).
Southern Methodist University

SMU Libraries SMU Perkins School of Theology



Design by Alicia Beebe

Printed in the United States of America

ISBN: 978-1-957946-15-3 (hard cover)
ISBN: 978-1-957946-14-6 (paperback)
ISBN: 978-1-957946-13-9 (open access)

*In memory of my parents,*
*Donald E. Binkley and Carolyn F. Binkley*

# CONTENTS

# FOREWORD

Although perhaps not well known today, in his time John Vincent was a well-known and popular protagonist in the shaping of modern American education and culture. For this reason, it does us well to remember him, and no one knows the career of John Vincent better than Tim Binkley, who correctly saw the value in collecting his reminiscences into a single volume. John Vincent's appealing voice and prolific pen went far to promote a national reconsideration of education, worship, and good citizenship. While innovative, Vincent was not a radical. He fit well within the emergence of a new urban middle class, which was striving at the end of the 19th century to attain greater sophistication while holding on to rural values and American identity.

His ideas were not based on theory, but on experience – his own experience. Looking back over his life, Vincent shares with his readers the events and lessons of his earlier years, which allows us to understand his thoughts in both a personal and historical context. He tells us how his rejection of rigid religious doctrine and ritualism grew from overcoming the religious terror he felt as a young boy during the years leading up to the 'Great Disappointment;'[1] and how this led him to turn to less severe approaches to faith, including those that regarded holiness as more than a

1. Editor's note: Concerning the Great Disappointment, in the 1840s many thousands of Americans were drawn to the end-times preaching of William Miller (1782-1849) who predicted that Christ's return would take place in October 1844. When that did not happen, the wide-spread heightened sense of religious anticipation collapsed. Out of the Great Disappointment came both a falling away from faith and the beginnings of several new end times-focused

doctrine, and that held up the good life as something much more than a safe passage to death. The lessons Vincent learned in his youth would guide him in his redesigning of the camp meeting and steer him away from temporary emotionalism in favor of a steady personal and social development through life-long learning and moral improvement.

Vincent's reflections also reveal the tensions and contradictions found in any creative mind. While rejecting the concentration on moral 'safety' in his early education, he continued to promote many of the good habits he had been taught; and, while his own education established in his mind the importance of home learning, he also regretted never having had the 'collegiate' experience. A reconciliation of these experiences can be found in his crafting of the Chautauqua Idea and Movement.[2] Regarding moral safety, Vincent advocated the good use of leisure over asceticism. Discipline and restraint were necessary, but not at the expense of leisure itself. At Chautauqua, leisure was not a license. Rather, it was Sabbath time – a time of rest in which one could appreciate the completion of work and the perfection of creation. Chautauqua's mission was to show people how to find and use this time, not just one day a week, but on every day throughout the year. Similarly, Vincent continued to revere the home as the best school, but he also appreciated the need for the classroom. Through the Chautauqua Literary and Scientific Circle, a four-year correspondence reading program created by Vincent in 1878, the home and

denominations, including the Jehovah's Witnesses and the Seventh Day Adventists.

2. Editor's note: A brief introduction to the Chautauqua Institution's mission and history is available at https://www.chq.org/about/. A detailed account can be found in Vincent's 1885 book, *The Chautauqua Movement*. That text is available at https://archive.org/.

the classroom were joined into one. The CLSC provided homes with the proper books and study guidance they needed to be good schools, along with the fellowship of other students. There had been correspondence courses before on specific subjects, but this course offered a general education in several subjects leading to what he called the 'college outlook;' and this, not only enriched the lives of its students, but it also made them more productive citizens and better teachers for their children.

Perhaps most of all, these reminiscences show how John Vincent from early childhood was a preacher and a teacher, which he believed to be one and the same. At the age of five, he was lecturing and preaching to his neighbors' enslaved children in Tuscaloosa, Alabama. At the age of 15, he was teaching school. Later, he went into business for himself having learned how to teach geography by singing. Soon, he found his way to the pulpit, first as a circuit rider and later as a pastor. He understood this was his calling and his talent, and he never stopped teaching and preaching whether in person or in writing. This was his life – a missionary charism to instruct people anywhere, at any social level and at any age about the word and works of God and mankind. This was not something he grew into. He did not become a teacher and preacher. He was born one.

I have been the Archivist and Historian for the Chautauqua Institution for over 20 years, and this book has brought me much closer to understanding its cofounder. I wish I had had it when I started.

*Jonathan David Schmitz*
*Chautauqua, New York*
*January 2024*

# INTRODUCTION

*"It does the living good to be reminded of the words and deeds of the worthy dead."*

John Heyl Vincent.

"The Autobiography of Bishop Vincent – Twelfth Paper."

This book is about a public figure whose name has been forgotten but whose legacy lives on. During his lifetime (1832-1920), John Heyl Vincent was known as an optimistic, world-traveling Methodist bishop who was an innovative educator, celebrated public speaker, and confidant of Ulysses S. Grant.[1] Many thousands of Americans read the periodicals that Vincent edited and the articles, booklets, and books that he wrote. Although he could and did preach, Vincent felt that his main calling in life was to teach. To that end, he became one of the driving forces behind the development of the modern Sunday school movement in the United States. As an experimental extension of that work, Vincent and another Methodist Sunday school man, Lewis Miller, established the first National Sunday School Assembly at Fairpoint, New York, in 1874. By popular demand, that educational gathering was repeated and enlarged, becoming today's Chautauqua Institution and an international life-long learning movement.

Surprisingly little was published about Bishop Vincent during the century following his death. The only full biography of Vincent

1. See chapter 25 ("The Autobiography of Bishop Vincent – Twenty-second Paper") for an outline of Vincent's extensive world travels.

was an informative but uncritical study written by his nephew, Leon H. Vincent, Litt. D., published in 1925.[2] Since that time, no other author has made the telling of Bishop Vincent's life story the primary focus of a book.

This volume is meant to fill that gap. However, it is not an exercise in analytical biography. The task at hand is to assemble the pieces of a fragmented, long-forgotten story as told by the main character. My hope is that this volume will allow readers to join Vincent in exploring his formative circumstances, proudest moments, and greatest regrets.

Are Vincent's recollections to be trusted? They are admittedly subjective and selective. Memory is a fragile thing. Self-aggrandizement is always a danger for writers. On the other hand, Vincent was a witness to his own life. Who else could have known the intimate details of his thoughts and feelings?

Leon Vincent's biographical sketch mentioned his uncle's "somewhat rambling" autobiography eighteen times.[3] Naturally, that raised my interest as I processed the bishop's personal papers in 2010. The discovery of hand-annotated proof pages in the Vincent collection launched a search of library catalogues. No library in the world claimed to own such a book. Then I found a proof page bearing the annotation "*Northwestern Christian Advocate.*" A

2. *John Heyl Vincent: A Biographical Sketch.* New York: The Macmillan Company, 1925. Now in the public domain, this work can be accessed online through https://archive.org. Many of the resources gathered by Bishop Vincent for his autobiography and by Leon H. Vincent (1859 – 1941) for his biographical sketch of the bishop are held in Southern Methodist University's Bridwell Library, Dallas, Texas. Bridwell Library is also the source of John H. Vincent's letter to Rev. William Wood, chapter 29 in this book.
3. A finding aid to the John Heyl Vincent papers is available online at https://txarchives.org/smu/finding_aids/00143.xml.

thorough examination of volumes of that Chicago-based Methodist periodical provided the answer. Vincent's autobiography was never published as a single volume. Instead, it was published between April and November of 1910 as a series of twenty-five essays ("Papers").

That "discovery" was followed by another: other researchers had previously solved the mystery. I was not the first. But from that moment I have wanted to turn Vincent's segmented memoirs into a monograph.

As this book was being envisioned, I identified additional autobiographical writings by John Heyl Vincent. Some were letters. Most were short essays published as booklets or articles. All merited inclusion in this book.[4] While a few stories and phrases are repeated, each document contains unique material. Within repeated passages, it is interesting to see how Vincent's recollections and interpretations of events changed over the course of years. To facilitate such observations, Vincent's writings are arranged chronologically in this volume.

Readers will note that the twenty-five-part official autobiography of John Heyl Vincent is not a linear recitation of his life story. Instead, it is a series of topical, semi-chronological, stream-of-consciousness memoirs that Vincent termed "pages of reminiscence."[5] Because Vincent's presentation is not linear, I have created a timeline of his life events as an aid to the reader.

4. In the booklet *In Search of His Grave,* An Easter Study (Flood and Vincent, 1893), pages 5-9, Vincent published recollections and reflections on his visits to the Holy Lands. Although this self-narrative is worth reading, it did not fit into the structure of the present volume.
5. John Heyl Vincent. "The Autobiography of Bishop Vincent – Fourth Paper," *Northwestern Christian Advocate,* May 10, 1910.

As Vincent wrote or perhaps dictated his essays, his focus shifted and drifted. In telling his own stories, Vincent often delved into the details of the lives of friends and associates who clearly meant a great deal to him. Vincent's encounters with scholars, preachers, and church members shaped his intellect and his life. With that in mind, something significant is missing from Vincent's autobiography. He barely mentioned the people closest to him: his siblings, wife, son, and Chautauqua Institution co-founder Lewis Miller.

Readers of this volume will discover that Vincent developed a keen interest in genealogy. He was not shy about sharing long-ago family history details. These passages could have been fodder for the editor's cutting block, but I chose to keep them. Such details were important to John Heyl Vincent's sense of self-identity.

A significant theme in Vincent's autobiographies is his spiritual journey from a childhood religion of fear and depression to a life-affirming faith that valued the here and now. This was not an easy transformation, but as you will read, he had many guides along the way, both in person and in print.

In the concluding paper, Vincent voiced the concern that his memoirs contained, "too much moralizing, too much preaching."[6] He was right. Clearly, Vincent needed an editor. Perhaps no one was willing to vex the bishop in that way in 1910. This editor has also decided to present Vincent's writings with a minimum of editing. Therefore, readers will encounter a few antiquated spellings and wordings amid a plethora of run-on sentences and mini homilies. These are not mistakes that need to be remedied. I invite

6. John Heyl Vincent. "Autobiography, Concluding Paper." *Northwestern Christian Advocate*, November 2, 1910.

you to think of them as indicative of Vincent's talkative personality and his primary mode of communication: oratory.

Although the Chautauqua experience of today differs from that of 150 years ago, Vincent's ideals continue to inspire. If you look for the pillars of Chautauqua in Vincent's writings, you will find them.[7] What you will not find in this book is an institutional history of Chautauqua. Vincent covered that topic in his 1886 book, *The Chautauqua Movement.*

Personally, I resonate with many of Vincent's visions for church and society, such as his convictions that education should not be limited by age, gender, or economic status, that learning is a quest that can uplift all of society, that the home is the most important school of theology, and that all of life is sacred: "We are to eat, to drink, to work, to think, for the glory of God whose we are and whom we serve."[8] On the other hand, I find some of Vincent's statements perplexing or offensive by today's standards. Take, for instance, his denunciation of slavery while, at the same time, perpetuating the "happy slave" ideology associated with his memories of early childhood in Alabama. These views are antithetical.[9] Another paradox is how Vincent's grand vision of ecumenical cooperation ("the Holy Catholic Church") contrasted with his anti-Roman Catholic rhetoric. Also troubling is Vincent's

7. The four pillars of the Chautauqua Institution are the arts, religion, education, and recreation. Source: https://www.chq.org/about/ accessed November 1, 2023.
8. John Heyl Vincent. "Autobiography, Fifth Paper." *Northwestern Christian Advocate,* May 4, 1910.
9. It is interesting to note that although Vincent only lived in Alabama for five years, he took pride in thinking of himself as a "son of the South." Vincent thought he could use this status to gain the support of Southerners for the Chautauqua Institution. The strategy was not very successful.

espousal of a form of civil religion in which Americanism is the highest form of Christianity and vice versa. Such conflations of church and state endanger the integrity of both institutions.

Bishop Vincent's memoirs include wit, conviction, and candor. His optimistic quest for the improvement of persons and society through education and religion reflect the Methodism of his era. Likewise, Vincent's linking of freedom with personal responsibility and his concern for making "religion a matter of everyday reality" are also deeply Methodist.[10] For those who may be unfamiliar with Vincent's Methodist Episcopal Church, I have added a brief essay on the topic as an appendix to this work.

While Vincent prized Methodism greatly, he did not view his faith tradition as the only valid way to practice Christianity. Instead, as a descendant of Huguenots, Quakers, Lutherans, and Presbyterians who was moved by the writings of Emanuel Swedenborg and other non-Methodists, Vincent gravitated toward inter-denominational work quite naturally.

In the twenty-first paper of his autobiography, Bishop Vincent wrote that "A great truth is greater when it has been looked at from two, three, or more sides." The immediate context for that statement was Vincent's appreciation of the diversity of Christianity. Based on the story of his life and the evidence of his work with the Chautauqua Institution, it is reasonable to believe that he applied this maxim to many other areas of life.

* * *

I would like to express my thanks to all who have made this work possible. First, I am profoundly grateful to my wife, Michelle

10. John Heyl Vincent. "Autobiography, Fifth Paper." *Northwestern Christian Advocate*, May 4, 1910.

Grimm, for the many hours she has invested in transcribing, proofreading, and discussing this text.[11] I also thank her for sharing my vision that Vincent should be enabled to speak again through his writings.

Thank you, Jon Schmitz, Historian and Archivist of the Chautauqua Institution, for providing a foreword to this book. I value you as a colleague and a friend. Your encouragement moved this project from initial research to completion.

The materials selected for this book were drawn from the archival resources of the J. S. Bridwell Library of Perkins School of Theology, Southern Methodist University, Dallas; the O'Brien Library of United Theological Seminary, Dayton, Ohio; and the Chautauqua Institution Archives. Thank you, Rebecca Howdeshell (Bridwell Library), Elisa McCune (Bridwell Library), and Andy Wood (O'Brien Library), for your invaluable research and scanning assistance.

I also wish to acknowledge historian Kent H. Roberts, Archivist of Highland Park United Methodist Church, Dallas, for his expert reading and advice. Finally, I want to thank Anthony Elia, Associate Dean of Special Collections and Academic Publishing and Director of Bridwell Library, for his enthusiastic support of this publishing project.

*Timothy S. Binkley*
*Berea, Kentucky*
*January 2024*

11. The articles by Vincent in this volume were transcribed from published copies.

# A TIMELINE OF EVENTS IN THE LIFE OF JOHN HEYL VINCENT

| | |
|---|---|
| **1821** | Parents Mary Raser and John Himrod Vincent married at Demopolis, Alabama. |
| **1832 February 23** | Born in Tuscaloosa, Alabama. |
| **1832 February 27** | Future wife Sarah Elizabeth Dusenberry born in Deposit, New York. |
| **1837** | Vincent family moved from Tuscaloosa, Alabama, to Chillisquaque, Northumberland County, Pennsylvania. |
| **1847** | Became a schoolteacher at the age of 15. |
| **1849** | Became an exhorter in his local church.[1] |
| **1850** | Licensed to preach. |
| **1851** | Assigned to assist the pastor of the Luzerne Circuit in Luzerne County, Pennsylvania. Luzerne was in the Baltimore Annual Conference of the Methodist Episcopal Church (MEC).[2] |
| **1852** | Both Ann Eliza Raser (orphaned cousin of Vincent adopted by his parents) and Mary Raser Vincent (mother of John Heyl Vincent) died at Chillisquaque within a period of three days. |

1. In Methodism and some other traditions, exhorters were proto-preachers who were authorized to practice public speaking by presenting short meditations.
2. MEC is used as an abbreviation for the Methodist Episcopal Church throughout this chronology and in foot notes throughout this work.

| | |
|---|---|
| **1852** | Attended Newark Wesleyan Institute one year while serving the Newark City Mission as preaching assistant. |
| **1853** | Entered the New Jersey Annual Conference of the MEC on trial. Appointed to serve the church in North Belleville (now Nutley), New Jersey. |
| **1855** | Appointed to serve the Camptown (now Irvington), New Jersey, MEC. |
| | Developed the "Palestine Class," an experiential Christian education program. |
| **1857** | Ordained an Elder in the New Jersey Conference of the MEC. Transferred to the Rock River Conference in Illinois. |
| **1857 – 1858** | Appointed to serve as pastor of the Joliet, Illinois, MEC. |
| **1858** | Married Sarah Elizabeth Dusenberry of Portville, New York. |
| **1859** | Appointed pastor of the MEC in Mt. Morris, Illinois. |
| **1860 – 1861** | Appointed to serve the Bench Street MEC in Galena, Illinois. |
| **1861** | Delivered a farewell address to Captain Ulysses S. Grant and the Jo Daviess County Guards as they departed Galena, Illinois, for the Civil War. |
| | Held his first Sunday School Institute in Freeport, Illinois. |
| | Book *Little Footprints in Bible Lands* published. |
| **1862** | Appointed to Third MEC, Rockford, Illinois, assisting Rev. William B. Slaughter. |

| | |
|---|---|
| **1862-1863** | Traveled to Europe and the Holy Lands. Attended the General Sunday School Convention in London as a foreign delegate. |
| **1863** | Served as pastor of Court Street MEC, Rockford, Illinois. |
| **1864** | Son George Edgar Vincent was born. |
| | Appointed pastor of Trinity MEC, Chicago. |
| **1865** | Met President Abraham Lincoln through General Ulysses S. Grant. |
| | Preached to Confederate prisoners at Libby Prison as part of his ministry with the U. S. Christian Commission. |
| | Appointed Sunday School Agent for the Rock River Annual Conference, MEC. |
| | Founded the periodical *Northwest Sunday-School Quarterly.* |
| **1866** | Appointed to head the Methodist Episcopal Sunday School Union in New York, New York. |
| | Founded the periodical *Sunday-School Teacher.* |
| | Booklet *The Sunday School Teachers' Institute* published. |
| **1868** | Appointed to serve the MEC as Corresponding Secretary of the Tract Society, Superintendent of the Department of Sunday School Instruction, and Editor of *Sunday School Journal.* |
| **1870** | Received an honorary Doctor of Divinity degree from Ohio Wesleyan University in Delaware, Ohio. |
| **1872** | Books *Sunday-school Institutes and Normal Classes* and *The Church School and Its Officers* published. |

| | |
|---|---|
| **1874** | Established the Chautauqua Lake Sunday School Assembly (forerunner of the Chautauqua Institution) with Lewis Miller. |
| **1875** | Received an honorary Bachelor of Arts degree from Mt. Union College in Alliance, Ohio. |
| | Orchestrated President Ulysses S. Grant's visit to the Chautauqua Institution. |
| **1877** | Booklet *Biblical Exploration or How to Study the Bible* published (Chautauqua text-books, no. 1). |
| **1878** | Established the Chautauqua Literary and Scientific Circle. |
| **1880** | Participated in the Centenary of Sunday Schools celebration in London, UK. |
| **1882** | Book *The Revival and After the Revival* published. |
| **1884** | Initiated the Oxford League as an attempt to draw young Methodists into a fellowship that valued university-level learning. |
| | Book *The Child's Bible* published. |
| **1885** | Received an honorary Doctor of Laws degree from Washington & Jefferson College in Washington, Pennsylvania. |
| | Founding editor of *Our Youth: A Paper for Young People and Their Teachers*, a weekly newspaper. |
| **1886** | Book *The Chautauqua Movement* published. |
| **1887** | Second trip to the Holy Lands. |
| | Books *The American Sunday School* and *The Modern Sunday School* published. |

## A TIMELINE OF EVENTS

| | |
|---|---|
| **1888** | Book *Better Not; A Discussion of Certain Social Customs* published. |
| **1888-1893** | Elected bishop in the MEC. His first episcopal assignment was to oversee the Methodist Episcopal churches of Western New York from Buffalo. |
| **1889** | The Oxford League and the Young People's Methodist Union merge to form the Epworth League. |
| | Book *The Church School and the Sunday-school Normal Guide* published. |
| **1890** | Books *Our Own Church* and *A Study in Pedagogy, For People Who Are Not Professional Teachers,* published; booklet *To Old Bethlehem* published. |
| **1892** | Booklet *My Mother; An Appreciation* published. |
| **1893** | Third trip to the Holy Lands. |
| | Book *The Church at Home: A Manual for Family Worship and Home Teaching* and booklet *In Search of His Grave, An Easter Study* published. |
| **1893-1900** | Second episcopal assignment in Topeka, Kansas. |
| **1896** | Received an honorary Doctor of Sacred Theology degree from Harvard University. |
| **1898** | Booklet *A Centennial Souvenir of John Himrod Vincent* published. |
| **1899** | Lewis Miller died in New York City at the age of 69. |
| **1900** | Book *The Inner Life; A Study in Christian Experience* published. |
| **1900-1904** | Final episcopal assignment was based in Zurich, Switzerland, leading the MEC's European conferences. |
| **1903** | Book *Chautauqua Hymnal and Liturgy* published. |

| | |
|---|---|
| **1904** | Book *Family Worship for Every Day in the Year* published. |
| **1909 March 31** | Wife Elizabeth ("Libby") Dusenbury Vincent died in Indianapolis, Indiana. |
| **1910** | *Northwestern Christian Advocate* published Vincent's autobiographical essays. |
| **1915** | Retired from Chautauqua Institution leadership. |
| **1920 May 9** | Died in Chicago at the age of 88. |

# Early Writings

1886 - 1898

## CHAPTER 1

# "How I Was Educated"[1]

***John H. Vincent,***
***Chancellor of Chautauqua University***
***1886***

MADAME NECKAR [sic][2] used to say, "It is never permissible to say, 'I say.'" The editor of *THE FORUM* does not accept this law, designed to protect society from the egotists; or else, with full knowledge of its wisdom, he has deliberately become accessory to its violation. He knows that the writers of the present series, and not the editor, must bear whatever penalty may be incurred.

In answer to a personal defense which I was once compelled to write in the interest of the Church I represented, my opponent reported the number of times I had in my article used the first personal pronoun; and, although this was no answer to my argument, it was quite successful in producing for a moment a feeling of mortification. What a harvest would my old antagonist find in the following pages were he disposed to continue the count! And

1. This work appeared in *The Forum*, June 1886, vol. 1, no.4, pages 337-347. It was also published as paper four in *"How I Was Educated" Papers from the Forum Magazine*. (New York: D. Appleton and Company, 1894.)
2. Suzanne Necker (also known as Suzanne Curchod, 1739-1794) was a Swiss writer and matron of the arts.

if Montaigne[3] is right when he says that "a man never speaks of himself without loss," I am certainly running great risk in accepting a commission to tell how I was educated, especially since the report I have to make is far from being creditable to myself, inasmuch as I never was "educated" in the sense in which the term is usually understood.

If the editor had asked, with that use of the perfect tense which embraces the past with an extension into the present, "How have you been educated?" or if he had asked, "How are you being educated?" I should have given – well, I shall avail myself of this opportunity for saying my say on the general subject of education, as I have come to look at it through a little over fifty-four years of the educational process; and shall try to show how I was delivered from the notion that education is principally a matter of schools and teachers, of text-books, tasks and recitation; and from that other notion that education belongs chiefly to the early years of one's life. Reminiscence does not bring my greatest joy as a student, for the present days are by far my best days, since in them I am learning more, and loving more to learn than ever before, since I opened my eyes on the morning of February 23, 1832, in the old town of Tuscaloosa, in the state of Alabama. The theory I have just advanced concerning the extent of the educational process, embracing as it does the whole of a life-time, will justify the wide autobiographical range which I take in the present article.

To state the matter fairly and fully at the outset, I must confess that I have never been at college. The reader can scarcely conceive the grief, made up of regret, discouragement, and mortification which this occasioned me through most of the years of my mature

3. French statesman, philosopher, and author Michel de Montaigne (1533-1592) popularized the essay as a literary genre.

life. Even now I sometimes feel the sting of it in the society of college men. It has been my "thorn in the flesh."[4] I have never found entire relief from its sharp prickings in the long list of distinguished men and women in both hemispheres and in all ages – writers, artists, sages, statesmen – who never enjoyed the benefits of college training; nor in recalling the melancholy failure in so many ways of so many men who have been matriculated, educated, graduated, and be-titled by the greatest universities; nor in the "practical" man's notion that classical education unfits a man for business. And certainly, I have never felt the comfortable self-complacency which is sometimes attributed to the self-educated man. The, to me, uncomfortable fact that I never even entered college, I have through all these years honestly faced and deeply deplored. The genuine regret which I have felt has supplied a large part of the conviction and inspiration under which I am now working for the increase of faith in the value of the college on the part of the average American citizen and parent. By voice, by pen, by example, in the ordering of my own son's education and by the Chautauqua service, I have for many years devoted my energies to the course of the higher education; and I make this statement concerning my relation to the college to place myself with the advocates of liberal culture as against the mistaken and mercenary theory of the utilitarian; and thus I make humble protest against the pitiable vanity of those self-educated men, who, not content with making boast of personal achievement, depreciate educational advantages which they failed to secure.

4. "Thorn in the flesh" is a phrase borrowed from 2 Corinthians 12:7 where the Apostle Paul wrote of having an affliction or impediment that was designed to keep him humble.

Of teachers and of schools, during my early years, I had many. My father was a man of large intelligence, a great reader, a good talker, a born debater, a man of sound sense, sterling integrity, strong religious convictions; of good old long-lived Huguenot stock, training his children to the highest family and social self-respect; tracing his ancestry to the south of France where my great-great-great-grandfather, Levi Vincent, was born April 10, 1676. In early life my father left his birthplace, Milton, Pa., and lived for many years in Alabama. There he met and married my mother – my first teacher, my best teacher, and the inspirer of my life even now, after these thirty-four years of silence. She was beyond most women in all the best qualities of motherhood, and to me, as Richter says, she "has made all other mothers venerable."[5] With Tennyson I can sing:

> "Happy is he with such a mother!
>
> . . . . . . . . .
>
> Trust in all things high comes easy to him."[6]

My earliest recollections of the formal educational methods are connected with a little private school in Philadelphia, kept by a good old woman whose name I have forgotten, under whose care I was placed for a few weeks in 1837, while the family were *en route* from Alabama to the Susquehanna Valley. Then came the administration of a governess, who taught my brother and myself daily in

5. German Romantic writer Johann Paul Friedrich Richter (1763-1825). The entire quotation is "Unhappy is the man for whom his own mother has not made all other mothers venerable."
6. From English poet Alfred Tennyson (1809-1892). The full stanza reads, "Happy is he with such a mother. Faith in womankind beats with his blood, and trust in all things high comes easy to him."

an upper room of our home on the side of Montour Ridge, near the mouth of Chillisquaque Creek, in Central Pennsylvania. She gave us lessons in reading, spelling, numbers, writing, history, geography, and manners. She was as good as we restless boys would allow her to be, and we cherish her memory to this day. How long this *regime* lasted I cannot now remember; but after it came several years of school-life in Milton Academy, the Lewisburgh [sic] Academy, the old "Sand Hill School House" at Chillisquaque, and the preparatory department of the Lewisburgh [sic] University, under dear old Doctor Taylor and his gifted son Alfred. Later on, I spent a year in Newark, N. J., at the Wesleyan Institute, which closed my career as a formal student in a regular institution.

During these school years I studied all that any boy under fifteen or sixteen was expected to study. I mastered Kirkham's "English Grammar," and Murray's also; I had all the definitions and rules at tongue's end, and much of the "fine print." I could parse glibly. I spent months in thus dissecting Milton's "Paradise Lost," and I nevertheless still revere the poem and its author. I was drilled in Town's "Analysis." I read and re-read the old "English Reader" and Porter's "Rhetorical Reader." I studied Latin in those days and knew the grammar well; translated the "Reader," "Cornelius Nepos," and "Caesar;" recited in Natural Philosophy (Comstock's), and in Chemistry and Astronomy. I wrote compositions and made declamations. I got along well with my teachers. They were, with a single exception, kind, and I was studious. I was not a remarkably bright or ready pupil, and, except under one teacher, was never, I think, accounted dull or slow. Of that teacher I have only this to say, that I have made the memory of his injustice and severity serve me well, as they have warned me against imitating him, and have enabled me to warn secular teachers by the thousand against the sad and inexcusable mistakes he made.

I taught school for several terms, beginning the summer that I was fifteen, in a little school-house near my father's house in Chillisquaque. My last school was at Mechanicsville, near Colraine Forge, in Pennsylvania, in 1850-1851. I loved dearly to teach and was myself a student while I taught. I may not here, for lack of space, recall the various devices by which I made school-life a pleasurable experience to my pupils and a means of discipline to myself. How well I remember the little grove (adjoining the old Watsontown school-house in Pennsylvania), a small section of which, in 1848, my pupils and I inclosed [sic] with a rustic fence and provided with seats, thus creating a miniature Chautauqua: there on pleasant days, in the open air, under the shade of the trees, amidst the singing of birds, we drank in the fresh air of heaven, and studied our lessons with renewed diligence.` The warm grasp of the hand and the affectionate allusion to the old school days which I occasionally receive from some former student, make me glad that I ever taught, and make me prize more and more the high, helpful, and holy office of the teacher. Through most of my career as a pastor – 1853 to 1865 – I kept up special classes in Biblical history, geography, and interpretation, and in Sunday-school normal work, prizing the service of teaching as a means of personal intellectual discipline. To teach honestly is to be a student, and that under most favorable conditions; for to teach, one must know; must know more than he expects to teach; must know how so to "put" knowledge as to bring others minds into a receptive and active state toward knowledge; and must himself feel that inspiration which comes from the contact between eager minds – minds eager to know and minds eager to quicken and to communicate.

The chief value of my almost continuous school-life as a student for the first fifteen years, and of my school-life as a teacher for nearly four years that followed, lay in my home-life and its rare opportunities. My father was a reader and had a small but valuable library which he required his children to use. I sometimes wish that I had owned Scott's writings in those days, but fiction was not heartily approved in the old home. I read "Robinson Crusoe" and the "Swiss Family Robinson," Bunyan's "Pilgrim's Progress" (which my father did not consider a work of fiction), and a few other products of the imagination; but I did read, and that before I was fifteen years of age, "The Spectator," Gibbon's "Rome," Rollin's "Ancient History," Pitkin's "Civil and Political History of the United States," Plutarch's "Lives," Pollock's "Course of Time," Young's "Night Thoughts," "Paradise Lost," Thomson's "Seasons," Cowper's "Task," Pope's "Essay on Man," and the general poems of Goldsmith. Among these my favorites were "The Spectator" and "The Seasons." I not only read but I studied them. Peter Parley's histories were far more pleasant and useful to me in those days than some of the statelier historical works I was required to read.

My father had given much attention to the matter of correct pronunciation and expression, and made a point of holding his children to the use of good English. All mis-pronunciations [sic] and all "bad grammar" which he detected were condemned, and we, the children, were not only allowed but encouraged to call attention to whatever we thought improper in the speech of each other, and of father himself. To this habit of parental carefulness, I owe more for what little knowledge of English I have than to all my teachers and text-books put together. Living for several years in a community where the worst provincialisms prevailed, I was kept to a great degree from falling into habits which it would have been hard in the after-years to correct.

The religious element was an important factor in my early training. My father was a strict disciplinarian and a firm Christian believer. Family prayer twice a day was the invariable rule. Sabbath was a day of public and domestic worship, of songs and prayer, and careful searchings of heart. The work of the week-day in school, in business, and in recreation was on the Sabbath brought to a rigid religious test. In all this there was no harshness or severity; it was simply placing emphasis upon the greatest reality of human life.

My mother was an incarnation of consistency, fidelity, self-sacrifice, and serenity. I never heard her speak one harsh or foolish word. She believed with her whole soul in the truths of religion as taught by Jesus of Nazareth, and her daily life was controlled by her faith. Therefore, I could never think of education as a mere disciplining or furnishing of the intellect. To my thought, it embraced the developing and ordering of the whole manhood. This was my mother's doctrine, continually reiterated by my father: education without religious faith and life is valueless. To my restless, undisciplined, selfish boy-nature, all this seemed hard and impracticable. To her it was easy, but it was beyond my grasp. Therefore, life was to me a struggle, full of divine aspirations and of all too human grovelings, of promise and of failure; and I suffered much from a conscious contrast between the best I dreamed of and the shabby best I did attain. False motives in study hampered me. It seemed to me that I had no right to gain mental power through selfish ambition. Education was my idol, and yet I could not conscientiously give myself wholly to it. In this atmosphere I was brought up, and my religious reading was determined by it. I read in my early boyhood (before I was fifteen) the lives of Harlan Page, John and Mary Fletcher, James B. Taylor, John Summerfield, John Wesley, William Carvosso, Adoniram Judson, and others of this saintly class.

Nature was full of wonder to me and wielded a strange influence over my life. The stars, the night-winds, the thunder, the clouds piled up like towers at the sunset, the ripples on the bosom of the river, the dark outline of the Montour Mountain in full view from my home; all these, and everything else in nature, took hold upon me, filling me with unrest and longing, that grew at times into a sort of torture. Everything had religious relations and intimations, and my young life during these earlier years was often morbid and sometimes wretched. I was exceedingly ambitious to be something in the world. I had a degree of faith in my ability, but eternity so impinged on the present as often to make life a melancholy thing. Legitimate recreation, not sufficiently encouraged by my father, seemed to me frivolity; my mother's saintliness all the while appearing as necessary as it was unattainable.

This chaotic religious condition may have been (I sometime think it was) a necessary step in my culture. I repeat the melancholy story not to condemn, but to make defense of early religious education, and to enter protest against the dangerous reaction of these latter days. I do not regret the faithful teachings which brought me thus early face to face with religious verities: but had this discipline lacked the demonstration of the pure and consistent life of my mother, it would have been disastrous in the extreme. Supported as it was by her living example, and by the real tenderness and integrity of my father, I was saved from permanent morbidness, and from the reaction which often comes to a man when the religious instruction of his youth has been a discipline of legality without love, and of dogmatism without the vitalizing and winning power of personal example.

I read in those days many sermons and much theology. I listened to lively discussions between Arminians and Calvinists, Baptists and pedo-Baptists [sic]; heard something of Second

Advent theories, and early began to prepare for the ministry to which my mother told me I had been at my birth consecrated.

In 1849 I was licensed to "exhort;" in the same year I received license as a local preacher; and in March, 1851, was appointed to serve as junior preacher on the Luzerne circuit in the old Baltimore conference, with a senior preacher, the Rev. John W. Elliott, in general charge of the circuit. In this my first year of service I did some of the most faithful study of my life. I was nineteen years old; college had been abandoned through the pressure of church influence and of personal conscientious conviction. Whatever I did must be done alone.

I rode on horseback over what was called a "four-weeks' circuit," extending from White Haven to Black Creek, a distance of thirty miles. Over the good roads which stretched across the mountains of this coal region I would ride for hours without seeing a house or meeting a traveler, and here I studied diligently. I perused my professional standard, the Holy Bible; read Watson's "Institutes" and Wesley's "Sermons;" prepared sermon-outlines of my own; practiced the delivery of them on horseback among the pines; committed to memory whole pages of Campbell's "Pleasures of Hope;" read the "Divina Commedia" of Dante; and studied every page of "The Methodist Quarterly," then edited by the scholarly John McClintock. I especially read and re-read the able series of papers on Comte's Positive Philosophy, which appeared that year in the "Quarterly." I wasted no time; I felt myself wholly unfit for the work I was engaged in; wondered if I could somehow manage to break loose from the holdings of what I believed to be Providence, and go to college; struggled day after day with my ambitions; recalled the words and looks of my mother; remembered what my father had written me in 1849: "I rejoice that you seem to have your mind fixed upon being something. Amen. Let it be something good."

I had as a public speaker an easy delivery, a good voice, and some pathetic power. My sensible father said to me before I left home: "Do not be deceived by the extravagant praise of weak and ignorant people, and especially of foolish women in the church. Remember how little they know, and what poor judges they are of preaching. Remember that back of the pleasant manner and good voice and correct pronunciation there must be sound thought." So, among those Pennsylvania forests I would read the articles on Conte's Philosophy, the book notices and editorials in the "Quarterly," and compare my sermons with the strength and wealth of thought, and the vigor of expression on those scholarly pages; and I often imagined John McClintock sitting behind me in the pulpit while I preached. This process not only kept me "humble" enough, but sometimes promoted a state of self-consciousness quite unfavorable to the most successful delivery of my sermons.

I made effort after effort to bring conscience and circumstances into line with my ambition, and to break loose from the active ministry in order to complete a college course. It was all in vain. I finally yielded, but it was after a prolonged struggle. Among my old letters I find two from my father written in 1852, in both of which he touches upon the great source of my trouble. He probes for motive. He urges me to do what seems best. "Could I have my mind fully satisfied," he writes, "that your aim is to glorify God in all this desire for knowledge, then I would say 'press toward the mark.' But if self stands out, then take care. You may become as 'sounding brass' or 'a tinkling cymbal,' with all your learning. Excuse this word of caution."[7] Later in 1852 he writes: "I notice your argument in favor of a learned ministry, but really, my son, the appeal is all labor lost. You are not one whit more in favor of a learned ministry than your father. All he objects to is a dependence upon learning." Here the father misunderstood the son, for the latter never for one moment placed the slightest dependence upon intellectual culture as a source of spiritual power. But it was something for a young man to have the frank, loving watch-care and counsel of so discreet and devoted a father.

The active ministry having been chosen, and all efforts to leave it even temporarily for further educational preparation having proven futile, in 1853 I joined the New Jersey Conference, and was appointed to my first church, at North Belleville, N. J., at the same time taking up the four years' course of preparatory study required by the Church: General history, the English branches, biblical, historical systematic, and practical theology, with written sermons and annual examinations.[8] Under this system in those days the candidate might by the grace of sympathetic examiners pass the examinations with comparative ease; but the man ambitious to do faithful work found such work possible, and from the beginning to the end of my four years' course I studied diligently, coveting the most rigid annual examinations that I might have the largest measure of self-respect as a student and prove to myself at least, what I might have done had the four years' college course been granted.

7. John Himrod Vincent's "word of caution" is couched in the language of 1 Corinthians 13:1.

8. North Belleville is now called Nutley, New Jersey. In Nutley there is a Vincent United Methodist Church.

During my early ministerial life, I conceived a plan reaching through the years by which, in connection with professional duties, I might turn my whole life into a college course, and by force of personal resolve secure many benefits of college education. I remembered that the college aims to promote, through force of personal resolve, the systematic training of all the mental faculties, to the habit of concentrated and continuous attention, that the mind with its varied energies may be trained and thus prepared to do its best work, subject to the direction of the will; that it cultivates the power of oral and written expression; that it encourages fellowships and competitions among students seeking the same end; that it secures the influence of professional specialists – great teachers who know how to inspire and to quicken other minds; that it gives to a man broad surveys of the fields of learning, discovering relations, indicating the lines of special research for those whose peculiar aptitudes are developed by college discipline; thus giving one a sense of his own littleness in the presence of the vast realm of truth exposed to view, so that he may find out with La Place that "what we know here is very little; what we are ignorant of is immense."[9]

The task before me was to secure these results to as large a degree as possible: mental discipline in order to intellectual achievement, practice in expression, contact with living students and living teachers, and the broad outlook which the college curriculum guarantees. This aim, therefore, for years controlled my professional and non-professional studies. It was constantly present in sermonizing, in teaching, in general reading, in pastoral visitation, in contact deliberately sought with the ablest men and women – specialists, scientists, *litterateurs*, whom I could find,

9. French scientist Pierre-Simon Laplace (1749-1827).

especially those who had gone through college or who had taught college. I secured from time-to-time special teachers in Greek, in Hebrew, in French, in physical science, giving what time I could to preparation and recitation. I read with care translations of Homer and Virgil, outlines of the leading Greek and Latin classics, and in connection with an exceedingly busy professional life, devoted much time to popular readings in science and English literature. When thirty years old I went abroad, and spent a year chiefly for the sake of coming into personal contact with the Old World of history and literature, and found double pleasure in the pilgrimage because I made it a part of *my* college training. In Egypt and Palestine, in Greece and Italy, I felt the spell of the old sages, writers, artists, and was glad to find that the readings of my youth and of my later manhood greatly helped me to appreciate the regions I visited and the remains in art and architecture which I was permitted to study.

This meager and somewhat morbid story of a half century of schooling has been told with perfect frankness. Since the struggles of those early years peace has come. The old and apparently irreconcilable conflict between studies secular and sacred has ceased. Life is no longer filled with insatiable longings. I am at school now as a student, every day; and unfinished *curricula* reach out into undefined futures. I shall never "finish" my education.

*John H. Vincent*

CHAPTER 2

# Excerpts from *My Mother: An Appreciation*

***1892***

For nearly forty years I have purposed, and again and again have begun, to tell the simple story of my mother's life. It is a story with not much, and yet with so much in it. Hers was not a long life. It ended at two score and nine years. But then it has not yet ended. Her personal influence remains to this day. To those who knew her, the mention of her name, even now, after forty years, brings the picture of a fair, sweet, illuminated face, a voice low and gentle, a bearing full of gracious dignity, and a life earnest, meek, unselfish, patient, spiritual, and abounding in the works of charity.

* * *

It was my mother's custom to retire from all other duties for about one hour every morning in order to read the Holy Scriptures and other books setting forth the Christian's inheritance in grace, and to pray for the divine support which she felt that she so constantly needed. The well-worn volumes of Christian biography which she read and re-read – the lives of Harlan Page, J. B. Taylor, Lady Huntington [sic], Carvosso, Lady Maxwell, Mary Fletcher – corroborate this interesting statement concerning her daily habit. No company, no domestic cares (the serious illness of her family alone excepted) could induce her to vary from this established order. Not that she ever made the slightest reference to it; but it was the habit of her life. She saved time and gained strength by retirement from the busy world. In this hour of prayer she saw the true meaning of life and the relative value of things temporal and things spiritual.

Her patience was wonderful. Acute pain she bore for years, but without a murmur. Never but once, and that was in my very early youth, do I remember seeing in her the slightest impatience, and then I was the sole cause. Too often, alas, through boyish carelessness and selfishness, and at that time especially, I was irritatingly rude. The manifestation of her vexation was very slight, but it grieved her to think that she had given expression even for a moment to her annoyance. Afterwards when we were together, she asked me to forgive her! Think of it! My mother (and such a mother!) asking *me* to forgive *her*! I never forgot that wonder of a mother's grace.

* * *

My mother was a rare teacher of her own children. She gave time to this work. Some writer says: "Stories first heard at mother's knee are never, wholly forgotten – a little spring that never quite dries up in our journey through the scorching years." There lies before me as I write an old book entitled "Illustrations of the Bible, by Westall and Martin," published in 1835, containing forty-seven fine steel plate engravings, with descriptive pages by the Rev. Robert Caunter, B. D. This is the picture textbook used at mother's knee – so long ago. There we gathered every Sunday to study the engravings, and under the witchery and power of her sweet voice to hear the full story told and to receive the applications which she made. Dear old, faded book! Sacred because of the divine themes it presents, but even more sacred to us because of the holy hands that held these pages before our youthful eyes, and because of the mother love that gave double force to the blessed lessons they contain.

* * *

Living as we did for several years two miles or more from the church, we did not usually attend evening service. But at home we always had, after tea, our evening song and prayer. For an hour or more we sang old hymns, revival and Sunday-school songs and sacred songs from an old book, "The Southern Harp," a collection of "original sacred and moral songs adapted to the most popular melodies, by Mrs. Mary S. B. Dana."[1] I can even now after all these years recall from the book "Soft, Soft Music is Stealing," as adapted to "Am I not Fondly Thine Own;" "Peace Be Still" to "Go Forget Me, Why Should Sorrow;" "Shed Not a Tear" to "Long, Long Ago;" "My Beloved Wilt Thou Own Me" to "Bounding Billows;" "I Have Heard, I Have Heard, I Have Known" to "Swiss Boy." Now and then my father would make a few earnest remarks suggested by the words we had sung. And there into the evening we sat singing and listening, and at last joining in prayer. The influence of those Sabbath evening song services follows her children to this day.

* * *

Beyond the "holy place" was the "holy of holies." For fifteen years it was my mother's invariable custom to take the children into her

1. Mrs. Mary Stanley Bunce Dana Schindler, a.k.a. "Mrs. Dana" (1810-1883) was a noted hymnodist, author, and editor. *The Southern Harp* was her first published book.

own room after the regular Sabbath even-song and service I have described. In the darkness, in the twilight, or in the moonlight we followed her. And there, seated together among the shadows, she would talk in her tender way about eternity and duty, about our faults as children, her anxiety about us, her intense desire for our salvation. She insisted upon the ethical side of religion: patience with each other, cheerful obedience to father, carefulness in our speech, honesty in all things. She recalled incidents of recent occurrence – quick words, signs of selfishness in the lives of her beloved children (and alas, how numerous they were!) which grieved her and made her anxious. Then we knelt together, and she prayed. And how she could pray! What fervor! What importunate faith! Oh, to hear again one of those Sunday evening prayers! Out of a soul burdened with sorrow for her children's defects, out of a soul filled with the burning love of God out of a life self-sacrificing and heroic and consistent came these wonderful appeals in behalf of her children. Living with God seven days a week, through all the weeks, when she brought us, her children, to the mercy-seat on the Sabbath evening, was not Heaven opened, and did not the place seem holy ground, and does any one wonder that her children cannot recall those scenes without a thrill of emotion and moistening eyes and a vow of renewed consecration?

* * *

Then came the night and silence and protecting wings of God's angels and the blessing of our mother's God hallowing the day, hallowing the house and making the memory of the Sabbaths of my childhood a means of grace, of penitence, of confession, of consecration, and of faith in the verities of the Christian religion which no arguments of the doubters can disturb. She walked with God. Believing in her, it was easy for those who loved her to believe in God.

* * *

When I was about sixteen years old, I left home for my first long absence. It was necessary to leave at midnight on the old-fashioned Pennsylvania packet boat. Father was absent in Philadelphia. It was the most dismal evening of my life. I dreaded the separation. Mother, feeling as keenly as her boy the pangs of the parting, did what kindness, self-control, and cheerful courage could to brighten the hours. More lamps were lighted. We played simple games, sang, talked, dreading and yet desiring for very love's sake that the clock would strike for midnight and the horn of the packet sound. The younger children tried to keep awake to the last, but it was impossible. They said, "good-bye to Brother John," and cried as if their little hearts were breaking. But sleep comforted them. And midnight came. And then the hurrying of luggage to the dock as the coming boat gave her signal. Then the good-byes to everybody but mother. "Don't cry when I start," I had said the day before. "I'll try to be brave, my boy," she said, "but it is hard to part." And when the parting came her face was very white and tears stood in her eyes. She put her arms around my neck, looked me in the face, kissed me again and again and said, "Good-bye, my son, live near to God, live near to God!" All that night I seemed to see the white face and to hear the holy words, "Live near to God."

Alas, dear mother, I have so often forgotten that solemn charge! But thank God the words are not forgotten, and through the boundless grace of my mother's God the opportunity has not been wholly lost!

* * *

Her last written words to me were dated January 4, 1852, a little more than six weeks before her death. I was then on my first circuit, "under the presiding elder," in Luzerne County, Pennsylvania. She was not able to finish the letter. But how significant and impressive are these last words! "Do you, my dear son, retire to your closet before and after you stand in the sacred desk to proclaim salvation to dying sinners? What a solemn, what a sacred office, to preach Christ and Him crucified! It seems to me that ministers, above all others, should be holy in heart and in life, always cheerful but never trifling, always kind and forgiving, careful not to wound the feelings of any, unless duty requires to reprove sin." What wisdom! What condemnation he feels to whom they were written!

CHAPTER 3

# Excerpts from *A Centennial Souvenir of John Himrod Vincent*

***Born in Milton, PA., April 20, 1798. Died August 13, 1873.***

*A very few copies are printed, and only for private use.*[1]

*1898*

THE VINCENTS are from an old French family. The name is Latin, and tradition carries it back to the fourth century. The *Bibliotheque Nationale,* on Rue Richelieu, in Paris, contains a long list of Vincents of various provinces and lines; Roman Catholic and Huguenot. On account of the bloody persecutions carried on against the Huguenots by the Papal power, as at the massacre on St. Bartholomew's Day, August 24, 1572, and on account of the Revocation in 1685, of the Edict of Nantes (issues in 1598), many Huguenots emigrated to England, Germany, the Netherlands, Switzerland, South Africa, and the North American Colonies. There are many Vincent families in England. Several large families of the same name in America came directly from France, some from England and some from France, via England and Holland.

1. This interesting line appears in print below the title in the original.

JOHN HIMROD VINCENT, the subject of this sketch, belonged to the family of LEVI VINCENT, who was born in Charente-Inferieur, on the coast of France, and probably in the Canton of Rochelle, in 1676. Immediately after the "Revocation" (1685) his family came from France for America and settled in New Rochelle, New York, and afterwards in New Jersey.

The line of descent is as follows: LEVI VINCENT, born in France, April 10, 1676; died in 1763. His wife's name was *Ester Debue*. The son of Levi was JOHN VINCENT, born January 26, 1709, on the farm where his father died. He married *Elizabeth Doremus,* December 1, 1773, and died February 24, 1801. Elizabeth Doremus was born July 13, 1711, and died February 11, 1788. She descended from Anneke Jans Webber, whose father was Wolpfert Webber. The family line reaches back to 1600.

The children of John Vincent and Elizabeth Doremus were Esther, Cornelius, Rachel, Elizabeth, Elizabeth (2d), Jane, Mary, Benjamin and Peter. The second son of John and grandson of Levi was CORNELIUS VINCENT, who was born on his father's farm in New Jersey, near Bloomfield, April 15, 1737. He married Phebe Ward in November, 1756; and died July 16, 1812, in Milton, Pennsylvania, at the home of his daughter Mary ("Aunt Polly Derickson"). The children of Cornelius Vincent and Phebe Ward were Isaac, Daniel, Bethuel, Sarah, Benjamin, John, Elizabeth, Rebekah and Mary. BETHUEL VINCENT, the third son of Cornelius, the grandson of John and great grandson of Levi, was born June 3, 1762, and died April 30, 1837. Major A. D. Mellick in his "Story of an Old Farm," says: "He was distinguished in his vicinity for the force and integrity of his character, his retentive memory and clear intellect; together with a robust and vigorous frame. He was postmaster at Milton for many years."[2]

The first wife of Bethuel Vincent, and who bore all his children, was *Martha Himrod*. She was the fourth child of Simon Ludwig Himroth (Himrod); born at Bedminster, N. J., October 12, 1764; married Bethuel Vincent, January 1, 1788; died August 10, 1806. Her father, *Simon Ludwig Himroth*, son of Wilhelm Himroth, was born in December 1731, at Bendorf, Germany; came to America in the ship "Two Brothers," landing at Philadelphia, September 15, 1752; joined his old friends, the Moelicks, at Bedminster, N. J.; married *Marie Catherine*, the sixth child of Johanne Moelick;* moved to Milton, Northumberland County, Pennsylvania, in 1772. Simon was member of the Pennsylvania Legislature from 1781 to 1785. The family line of the Moelicks runs back to the year 1500. The children of *Bethuel Vincent* and *Martha Himrod* were Sarah, William, Daniel, Mary, Benjamin, John Himrod, Phoebe, Phoebe (2d) and Martha.[3]

* * *

JOHN HIMROD VINCENT, the sixth son of Bethuel, grandson of Cornelius, great grandson of John and great grandson of Levi, was born in Milton, Northumberland County, Pennsylvania, April 20, 1798, and died in Erie Pennsylvania, twenty minutes before midnight, August 13, 1873. He left Milton, Pennsylvania, for the South

2. Andrew D. Mellick. "The Story of an Old Farm: Or Life in New Jersey in the Eighteenth Century." *Unionist-Gazette*, 1889.
3. At this point in the original text, the following footnote appeared: "The wife of Johanne Moelick and the mother of Marie Catherine was Marie Catherina, daughter of Burgomaster Gottfried Kirberger, of Bendorf. I have the copy of the baptismal certificate recording the fact and details of the baptism in the "Evangelical Head Church, by the Rev. Johannes Reasch, January 8, 1698."

with his brother-in-law, Major Hogan, of the U. S. [Army], August 25, 1819. He married Mary Raser at Demopolis, Alabama, September 6, 1821. She was daughter of Captain Bernard Raser, who died in the East Indies. The father of Bernard was Baltus Raser, whose marriage certificate (written and signed according to the custom of the "Friends"), bearing the date February 6, 1743, is still in the possession of the family.

Mary Raser (my mother) was born in Philadelphia, July 30, 1803, and died at Chillisquaque, Northumberland county, Pennsylvania, February 16, 1852. Her children were: (1) *Mary Amanda,* born at Tuscaloosa, Alabama, January 20, 1823; died October 12, 1823. (2) *William Raser Colgin,* born at Tuscaloosa May 11, 1825; died at Columbia, Miss., Nov. 6, 1825. (3) *Martha Ann,* born at Mobile, Alabama, March 13, 1828; died at Mobile, March 20, 1828. (4) *George Strothers Goins,* born at Demopolis, September 26, 1829; died at Demopolis, October 15, 1829. (5) *John Heyl,* born at Tuscaloosa, February 23, 1832.[4] (6) *Bethuel Thomas,* born at Tuscaloosa, August 9, 1834.[5] (7) *Frank Lyon,* born at Chillisquaque, Pennsylvania, February 28, 1839; died at Clifton Springs, New York, May 12, 1889.[6] (8) *Thomas Raser,* born at Chillisquaque, September 1841; died 1843. (9) *Mary Elizabeth,* born at Chillisquaque, June 9, 1842.[7]

4. John Heyl Vincent was the fifth child born in his family and the first to survive into adulthood.
5. Younger brother Bethuel Thomas Vincent (1834-1920) also became a Methodist minister. He served as the third president of Colorado Seminary (Iliff School of Theology).
6. Younger brother Dr. Frank Lyon Vincent (1839-1889) was a physician. He began his practice in Galena, Illinois, when John Heyl was serving as a pastor there.
7. Younger sister Mary Elizabeth Vincent Farovid (1842-1924) was married to James A. Favorid. After her husband's death in 1903, she lived in Bishop Vincent's home until his death in 1920.

* * *

My father was married the second time, June 2, 1853, at Erie, Pennsylvania, to Miss Ann Richards[8]. Her children – all born in Chicago – are (10) *Charles Richards*, born October 5, 1854.[9] (11) *Harry Collier*, born December 26, 1855.[10] (12) *Nellie*, born August 4, 1858; died October 5, 1863. (13) *Anna Dobbins*, born July 19, [1860][11]. (14) William Vincent, born March 8, 1862.

* * *

My father was a reader from his early years, interested in national affairs and devoted to Bible study and Sunday-school work. He was a superior superintendent, sometimes having charge of two-a morning school in the town and one in the afternoon in the country neighborhood where we lived. For years he rode two and a half miles to open his Sunday-school at 9 o clock. Many a time I found him by lamplight on Sabbath morning preparing his lesson for that day.

His library was not large but select. The old books are still with his children-The American Encyclopedia (thirteen volumes, I think), Shakespeare, Milton, Bunyan, The Spectator, Plutarch's Lives, Gibbon's Rome, Pitkin's Civil and Political History of the United States, Lardner's Outlines, Rollin's Ancient History, Thomson's Seasons, Pollock's Course of Time, Hervey's Meditations, Sturm's Reflections on the Works of God, Clark's Commentary,

8. Ann (or Anne) Richards Vincent (1823-1905).
9. Half-brother Charles Richards Vincent (1854-1937).
10. Half-brother Harry Collier Vincent (1855-1928).
11. Half-sister Anna Dobbins Vincent Massey (1860-1903).

Benson's Commentary, Wesley's Works, Memoir of James Brainerd Taylor, the lives of Carvosso, John and Mary Fletcher, etc.

He was an attractive man – social, genial, full of humor, considerate of others, magnetic and sympathetic. He had rare insight into human nature. He was most hospitable, an entertaining talker, fond of debate on political and religious subjects, a superior Sunday-school teacher and superintendent, and a most edifying class-leader. He was a fine singer. We always sang at family prayer, which was observed in the home of my childhood and youth twice every day, and our Sabbath home even-song was full of spiritual power. There we all joined in hymns and spiritual songs-the old and the new. ...These hours of song were interspersed with remarks and prayers in the twilight or moonlight and the memory of them fills life now with sweetness and hope.

As a father, he was almost perfect. He was firm, frank, faithful, just, tender; sometimes severe, but careful not to reprove or punish in anger. He was devout and conscientious, true to the core and although he suffered from business troubles and was in his later years much depressed, his trust in God was unwavering. One who knew him well in the later years writes: "How glowing his faith became and how beautiful were the years of his second childhood, in the feebleness of his body and the simplicity of his faith." He was for the last fifteen years of his life a victim of trembling palsy[12]. For a time he suffered greatly but he became less and less sensitive to his immediate surroundings. For several days at the last he became unconscious and finally slept away in one of the quietest slumbers. Several times during the last forty-eighty[sic] hours he smiled very sweetly. On the last Sunday when "Rock of Ages" was sung he tried to sing the bass. Cousin Martha Himrod

12. Now called Parkinson's Disease.

(Uncle Daniel V.'s daughter), Mrs. Richards, Eleanor Richards, Ma, Clarence and Harry were present. As father breathed his last, we all kneeled in prayer remembering the absent ones. He was buried at Erie, Pa., on Saturday, at 4 P. M.

Dr. Anson West in his history of "Methodism in Alabama," pages 319-322, gives this pleasant testimony:

Two honored names- John H. Vincent and Mary Vincent were entered on the Register of the Methodist Episcopal Church at Tuskaloosa [sic] at an early day, possibly as early as 1822. They lived in Tuskaloosa in 1822, '23,'24; and in Mobile in 1825, '26 and '27, and again in Tuskaloosa from at least the latter part of 1830 till the latter part of 1837, when they moved to Pennsylvania. . . . The name of John H. Vincent stands on the oldest Methodist Church Register for Tuskaloosa now extant. As a Steward, a Trustee and a member of the Building Committee, he filled at the same time these three important offices of the church, and with his associates in office, managed the financial affairs of the Methodists of Tuskaloosa; superintended the construction of their house of worship and held the property in trust for the congregation. In the supervision of the temporal affairs of the church he was a valuable member and in Sunday School work he was quite useful. In that work he was versatile and skillful, full of tact and a good talker. He was an earnest, faithful Christian. His ideal of Christian character was one of rare excellence. He regarded the Christian ministry as of divine appointment and questioned the motives of the minster of the gospel who proposed to turn aside from his holy calling to engage in secular pursuits. He maintained religion in his home. He had family prayers twice a day and carried his children with him to public service. Among the intimate friends of John H. and Mary Vincent in Tuskaloosa, were the preachers who had charge of the station, Henry W. Collier, Mary A. Collier, Alfred Battle,

Millicent Battle, James Guild, David and Stella Scott. Vincent will be perpetuated in Tuskaloosa where they were first initiated into the Methodist Episcopal Church.

# The Autobiography of Bishop Vincent

1910

CHAPTER 4

# The Autobiography of Bishop Vincent

## First Paper[1]

*April 6, 1910*

The Vincents came from France. The name is Latin and tradition carries it back to the fourth century. The *Bibliothèque Nationale,* on Rue Richelieu, in Paris, contains a long list of Vincents of various lines and from various provinces. They represented both Roman Catholic and Protestant faiths.

On account of the bloody persecutions carried on against the Huguenots by the papal power, as at the massacre on St. Bartholomew's Day, August 24, 1572, and on account of the revocation in 1685 of the Edict of Nantes (issued in 1598) many Huguenots emigrated to England, Germany, the Netherlands, Switzerland, South Africa, and the North American colonies. Several families of Vincents came directly to America from France, and some by way of England and Holland.

The line of descent, in which at this writing we are interested, is through Levi Vincent, who was born in Charante Inférieure, on the west coast of France and probably in the canton of Rochelle, April 10, 1676. He died in 1763 in New Jersey, to which state he had moved from New Rochelle in New York. The wife of Levi Vincent

1. *Northwestern Christian Advocate,* Vol. 58, No. 14, pages 12-13.

was Esther Debue. The son of Levi and Esther was John Vincent, who was born January 26, 1709, on the farm in New Jersey where his father died. John married Elisabeth Doremus, December 1, 1733, and died February 24, 1801. Elisabeth Doremus was born July 13, 1711, and died February 11, 1788. She descended from Anneke Jans Webber, whose father was Wolpfert Webber. That family line reaches back to 1600. And just here our trustworthy antiquarian finds a crown and a scepter, very nice relics to preserve, but being genuine republicans, we shall leave them where we found them.

The children of John Vincent and Elisabeth Doremus were Esther, Cornelius, Rachel, Elisabeth, Elisabeth (second), Jane, Mary, Benjamin, and Peter, all biblical names but one, as will be seen. Cornelius Vincent, the second son of John and grandson of Levi, was born on his father's farm in New Jersey, near Bloomfield, April 15, 1737. He married Phebe Ward, in November 1756. Their children were Isaac, Daniel, Bethuel, Sarah, Benjamin, John, Elisabeth, Rebekah, and Mary – good Scripture names for an old-fashioned Hugenotic family! Bethuel Vincent, son of Cornelius and Phebe, grandson of John, and great-grandson of Levi, was my grandfather. He was born June 3, 1762, and died April 30, 1837. Major A. D. Mellick, in his interesting "Story of an Old Farm" says of my Grandfather Bethuel: "He was distinguished in his vicinity for the force and integrity of his character, his retentive memory, and clear intellect, as well as for his robust and vigorous frame. He was postmaster at Milton for many years."

And a word about my grandmother is not out of place just here. She was his first wife and bore all his children. She was the fourth child of Simon Ludwig Himroth (Himrod); born at Bedminster, N. J., October 12, 1764; married Bethuel Vincent January 1, 1788; died August 10, 1806. Her father (Simon) was a member of the Pennsylvania Legislature from 1781 to 1785. The family record of the Moelicks runs back to the year 1500. The children of Bethuel Vincent and Martha Himrod were Sarah, William, Daniel, Mary, Benjamin, John Himrod, Phoebe, Phoebe (second), and Martha. John Himrod Vincent, my father, the-sixth son of Bethuel, grandson of Cornelius, great-grandson of John, and great-great-grandson of Levi, was born in Milton, Northumberland County, Pa., April 20, 1798, and died in Erie, Pa., August 13, 1873.

### *Blood Will Tell*

A wholesome family pride has educating power in it. Children should be brought up to look up the family record. And if there be nothing much to begin with, a family enthusiasm and ambition may easily be kindled. If father, mother, and their children have little to look back at, they have a future packed with possibilities. And the beginning of all family life that is worth while [sic] is in ambition, faith in God, and firm resolve. A few rules of life, a few radical mottoes chosen as the watchwords of the household, a collection of pictures to be studied, a few strong books read aloud in the evenings, a little home journal conscientiously kept, the observance of family days – birthdays, days marking important events in the family history – the love of music, the fine art of story telling [sic], the frequent half hour of humor, a few lively games, the spirit of hospitality reaching out after friends and neighbors too much neglected by the Church and other people – and soon our plain little home has enthusiasm, hospitality, the high art of laughing, abounding good will, and for more than one generation memories full of quickening power will linger long after father and mother have gone to the blessed land of which their home has been a type and foretaste.

The Vincents moved to Pennsylvania in 1772 from Newark Township, Essex County, colony of New Jersey, where Bethuel Vincent, my grandfather, was born. They settled near the mouth of Warrior Run Creek, north of Milton. Here Cornelius built a grist mill. It was in the same year (1772) that Northumberland County was organized.

## *Early Settlement*

It was in the summer of 1778 that the Indians and the English attacked the white settlers on the west branch of the Susquehanna. The Freelands and the Vincents were compelled for a time to abandon their homes. They returned later in the season. It was then that Jacob Freeland, Sr., built himself a new, large, and substantial two-story log house near to his saw mill, and surrounded the house with a fence twelve feet in height. Within this inclosure [sic] he lived. This was afterward known as Fort Freeland, not more than a mile from the present Warrior Run Presbyterian Church.

In the autumn of 1778 the following thirteen families united for mutual protection against the English and the Indians: Jacob Freeland, Sr., Jacob Freeland, Jr., Michael Freeland, John Vincent, James Durham, Samuel Gould, John Lytle, Moses Kirk, and George Pack. The Indians and British took Michael Freeland and Daniel Vincent prisoners. Bethuel Vincent, my grandfather, was then a mere lad. He also was taken captive and sent to Canada, where he was held for months and where he learned to speak French. It is reported that Daniel escaped from the British by killing two Indian boys who were placed over him as a guard.

It was on Wednesday, July 28, 1779, that Captain John MacDonald of the British Army, at the head of about one hundred regulars and two hundred Indians, surrounded Fort Freeland, and captured it. As the fort had but a small supply of bullets when the battle began, Phoebe Vincent (the wife of Cornelius) and Mary Kirk (the wife of Moses Kirk) began to melt the pewter plates, dishes, and spoons in the fort, and ran them into bullets for the use of the men. MacDonald sent a white flag three times into the fort demanding surrender. At last, after his threat of setting fire to the fort and massacring every person within it, they surrendered, and the fort was captured by his majesty's troops. The men bearing arms were sent as prisoners to Fort Niagara. The women were not molested but allowed to go down to the river as they pleased. Squire J. F. Wolfinger of Milton (to whom I am indebted for the chief details of the battle) says that as the women were not deprived of their clothing they filled their pockets with the finest and most valuable of their belongings, put on two or three suits of apparel, dressed their boys and girls in similar manner, and allowed them to move down the country wherever they chose to go.

CHAPTER 5

# The Autobiography of Bishop Vincent

# Second Paper[1]

*April 13, 1910*

Of my birthplace, Tuscaloosa, Ala., I have but the faintest recollections. I remember the broad piazza that surrounded the large, low, one story house in which we lived, and I can see on a day of rain the drops falling into the little pools of water in the yard, each drop as it fell becoming what seemed like a tiny fountain until the whole yard seemed to be a lakelet with a thousand little fountains at play, and the music of the waters I can remember to this day. It was a pleasant home and the slight recollections still give pleasure – the bright sunshine, the pleasant trees, the tender and loving mother, the father interested in us and our play, the good "mammy" with her skin of ebony, tall Eliza a mulatto servant, who seemed to me "so very tall," and "Primus," a black servant, very black and very good-natured. I remember a "runaway match" that about that time gave at first a bit of fun and later on a touch of solicitude when Harriet Scott, my next door neighbor and constant playmate and of about my age, ran off with me one day and we traveled out to the university

1. *Northwestern Christian Advocate*, Vol. 58, No. 15, pages 12-13.

where we went to see our good friend, Professor Tutwiler[2]. He was my Sunday School teacher and both Harriet and I knew the way and reached the professor's house. But soon we saw a messenger making for us. It was Eliza with a long stick in her hand. She wore a feigned frown, but it was like a very thin veil over a smiling face. And we read the situation at once. I remember distinctly what I thought as she approached us with a threat and a gesture. I said to myself, "She doesn't dare to touch us with that rod." But it was Eliza's purpose that the two little white runaways should say good-by [sic] to their temporary hosts and make for home. Harriet and I were "freshmen" indeed but too young for matriculation. And neither she nor the professors of the university were as yet converted to the modern doctrine of "coeducation," and I am not sure at this writing that the present university authorities have been converted to it. And my dear friend, Miss Frances Willard, in the days later on, when she and the writer discussed, in good humor, the "woman question" and the open college for both sexes, would certainly have seen in that little runaway couple en route for college a prophecy of the "good times" when men and women should enter and together pass through the universities. There was a time when I hesitated to say "Amen" to this proposition, but even old men may grow in both knowledge and grace. I have increasing faith in the breadth of woman's sphere and in "adult education."

2. Professor of Ancient and Modern Languages Henry Tutwiler (1807-1884) was a founding faculty member of the University of Alabama.

## SECOND PAPER

### *Early Associations*

Harriet Scott, my constant playmate in those earliest days, afterward became the wife of Bishop Hargrove of the Methodist Episcopal Church South. , Her mother was my own mother's most intimate friend in the South. Mrs. Scott was a New England woman, a Massachusetts "school marm," a Miss Houghton, sister, I think, of the head of the old firm of Houghton & Mifflin.

In those old Tuscaloosa days I took my first lessons in Church-going. It was the theory of my parents that little children should always attend the public services of the Church, especially on Sunday morning; that Sunday School is never intended to be a substitute for attendance upon the public service and that if a boy of five can attend but one service on Sunday, the public service or the Sunday School, by all means let it be the public service. And if parental authority requires it, pastoral wisdom ought to contribute to its attractiveness and effectiveness by promptness, compactness, and brevity in the ordering of the public service, and especially in that part of the public service known as the sermon and over which the preacher is supposed to have absolute control. And nine times out of ten that function should be limited to three times ten minutes.

I left Tuscaloosa with my father and mother in 1837, I think it was. And when in about 1871 I visited the old city of my birth, when once I was shown the way to the Church I had attended I was able to move in the right direction to find the house in which I had lived. It is a good thing to train children to attend the public services especially on every Sunday morning. It is an excellent thing to have home and Church made one in the child's mind.

### *Removal to Pennsylvania*

My mother was not happy in the South, chiefly on account of slavery and father decided to return from the South to his old home in Pennsylvania. I was at that time between five and six years of age. We had already made a journey to Philadelphia and Milton on the Susquehanna where my grandfather lived. It was not as easy in those days to make long journeys as in our times. We had to depend on old-fashioned steamboats, more uncomfortable stage coaches, and on one of our northern trips made a large part of the journey in a carriage. But we were children, fond of change, delighting in the new experience of going day after day, now through forests, now over the mountains, stopping for rest at night at hotels, and occasionally using a steamer for the sake of variety and for the resting of our horses. It was a great treat to see our good old grandfather and the kindest of friends in my mother's old home in Philadelphia. We were carefully trained as children, father being firm in requiring prompt obedience and mother as tender as a mother ever was, often saying, "I am afraid we are indulging the children too much." It was our conviction as children that we were rather strictly brought up and restrained much more than many of the children I knew. But as I review those earliest years, I am very confident that few children have ever been more carefully trained in habits of obedience to parental authority nor more blessed with maternal example.

### *Childhood Religion*

Self-sacrifice in the children's interest and utmost fidelity to their spiritual well-being – these were the most prominent features in the domestic administration. Then there was reverence for the Sabbath that sometimes seemed a burden, but so strong was the everyday emphasis in our home on the religious factor in life that the Sabbath seemed to us children not only perfectly natural but a necessity. If religion has so much to do with everyday life how important it is to have one day out of the seven devoted to the studies, the devotions, and the self-restraint which have so much to do with earnest life on week days. The change of occupation, the special preparations on Saturday night, the silence of the Sabbath morning, the enforced attendance on the public service (so much a habit that nothing else was dreamed of), the reading of religious literature even by the children and then at eventide after the supper was over the retirement of the children to "mother's room" for special and most impressive conversation and prayer.

I well know how we have in our busy and secularized age allowed the Sabbath to drop into lower levels of a wholly secular life. To go to "Church," to attend "Sunday School," to visit and have "a good time" and to sneer at the old Puritans for their "rigidity" and "severity" and "narrowness" – these are alarming features of our age and augur ill for the Sabbath and the Church life of a decade hence. When I remember the "call" of the breakfast bell on Sunday morning at as early an hour as on any weekday morning, and the family prayers (with the singing of a Church hymn, the reading of a chapter from the Bible, and then the devout prayer of the "head of the family"), and as I remember how the books to be read on Sundays were chiefly of a religious character and designed to develop a sensitive and intelligent conscience, and how as a matter of duty everybody, all members of the family, were required to attend the regular Church service, I am compelled to wonder if we really appreciate the loss our Christian civilization has sustained by the substitution of indifference for reverence and of a conscience "dead to the demands, the positive commands of God concerning the "Holy Sabbath." This emphasis

I owe to the example and the administrative policies of the home of my childhood. And there is a positive "Thus saith the Lord" to justify this policy.

### *A Mother's Influence*

When religion is a reality in the faith and habits of parents, the children will grow up to regard it as a reality. They may refuse to be controlled by it in later years, but in the latest years they will have convictions which no form of doubt can weaken. And the sincerity of their parents can never fail to command their respect, and the probability is that at the last they will frankly confess the Christ who has followed them all the years.

Of the various forms of teaching nothing tells like unconscious influence. It is the most irresistible of all the forms which truth can assume. It is silent and undemonstrative, but it is unanswerable and effective. And the most favorable field for this potent teaching agency is the domestic circle. And it was with this conviction that my mother and her intimate friend, Mrs. David Scott of Tuscaloosa, used often to meet for conversation and prayer, their chief burden being the religious training of their children. They read such literature as the times furnished, conversed freely about the little everyday problems arising in connection with home administration. I sometimes wonder whether in our age with the new and pressing problems which the more complicated civilization in the heart of which we are living and the enlarging sphere of woman have developed, we are facing the situation and doing as parents all that might be done and that must be done to make home the power it needs to be in our times.

Formal and systematic education commands the attention of all classes in modern times. Libraries abound, lecture courses are popular, reading circles are found in every community, young people's societies develop enthusiasm among our adolescents, ministers and secular educators combine to create enthusiasm in popular education, but never so greatly have our homes and Churches needed the parental conscience and enthusiasm in the cause of religious education.

Of all forms of conversation none is more attractive and effective than that of mothers intent on the true training of their children, applying the latest psychological and the best pedagogical suggestions of this educational age to the noble work of training up their children in the nurture and admonition of the Lord.

In this noble age of woman's liberty, woman's exaltation, woman's opportunity – blessed is the woman who brings to the ministry of her enthusiastic and conscientious motherhood all the best things that art and science and literature and religion provide for her.

CHAPTER 6

# The Autobiography of Bishop Vincent

# Third Paper[1]

*April 20, 1910*

Although I spent but a short time – possibly not more than six years of my life in Alabama, I have always felt a measure of pride in the fact that I was "born in the South." There are many charms in Southern life. In spite of the blight of slavery it was a delightful region to live in. The climate is charming. Southern people have always been noted for their hospitality. They are cordial in manner and thoroughly "at home" in society. Slavery made it easily possible for them to entertain guests. The servants, many of them perfectly contented and happy, devoted to their mistresses, took pride in serving visitors and in demonstrating the skill and the resources of the family as hosts. They felt themselves to be a part of the family.

Slavery, an evil thing in itself, had its advantages in guaranteeing to the masters and their families large leisure, in fostering a refined and elegant social life, and it gave opportunities for the expression to their servants of genuine sympathy, so that in many respects the lives of the slaves were more secure and happy and reverently religious than if they had been entirely dependent upon

1. *Northwestern Christian Advocate,* Vol. 58, No. 16, pages 12-13.

themselves. The servants were often and generally cared for and appreciated, as though they were members of the family. Leisure and laziness do not always go together. As Benjamin Franklin said, "A life of leisure and a life of laziness are two things." The former encourages hospitality, which to the born Southerner is one of the fine arts. The changes which the war of 1861-65 effected in the South have not impaired the warmth and charm of the domestic welcome one finds as to-day he enters a really Southern home.

I happened to be in Richmond in 1865 as a visitor in the service of the Christian Commission on the day after the capture of the city. I met several Southern men and women, Confederates to the core, and they knew me to be a Northerner, and yet I was treated with the utmost kindness and consideration. Accepting the result of the war as in harmony with the divine purpose, they honestly tried to be reconciled to what was nevertheless to them a great disappointment, and they were as kind to me as though they had been of the North or I of the South.

It is not an easy thing for a people as a whole to be thoroughly fair while the politicians are seeking some advantage to be gained through the exciting of political animosities and local prejudices. But in the long run truth triumphs, and good will prevails. The best interests of both sections are promoted by silence, patience, and charity. We are one people. More and more has the sectional feeling subsided and it is the duty of every American to contribute as much as possible to the development of a just and at the same time a generous spirit.

Going back to the beginnings of my life I recall the final journey of our family to the North in the early forties. We came most of the way by private conveyance. A few pictures remain in my memory of carriage and coach and steamer experiences; Sunday rest in hotels *en route;* the frowns of a passenger on, I think, a

Cumberland River steamboat as I, a restless and busy boy, worked myself about the deck in a wooden box I had found. And I recall my feeling of resentment and defiance as I kept at my annoying, but to me enjoyable sport in spite of his unsyllabled protest. I recall the weariness of stagecoach travel, the comfortable rest at hotels here and there, the welcome of the Heyls in Philadelphia, and of my dear, old, white-haired grandfather in Milton. I vividly recall the ride from Milton down to Chillisquaque where we were to live; the well-wooded and to my child mind the lofty and mysterious Montour Ridge or mountain back of our house; the winding and beautiful Chillisquaque Creek, with its picturesque stone bridge – all these features made a distinct impression upon my mind and remain a delightful picture.

My father's niece, Elisabeth Brown, who afterward married my mother's brother, accompanied us from Alabama. She was a fine pianist, and soon after we settled in the new home a piano arrived from Philadelphia, and I well remember what delightful music my skillful cousin used to give us, and, as we could all sing, we spent many an evening through those earlier Chillisquaque years in services of instrumental and vocal music.

As the town where our church stood was nearly three miles away from our home, after attending public services in the morning we usually spent the evening in our own home in song services which sometimes lasted two hours or more. We sang together the old Church hymns, revival melodies and choruses, and occasionally made our selections from a collection of sacred songs adapted to the popular secular music of the times. Of these we were especially fond. We could all sing, after a fashion, and thoroughly enjoyed these Sunday evening home concerts. Father would now and then emphasize the sentiment of a hymn we had just sung and at the close of our little home song-service we would all kneel while father offered a prayer. Mother also sometimes prayed.

It was father's invariable custom to have family prayer every morning and every evening; and it was not in either case a hurried service. There was always the reading of a Scripture selection, the singing of a hymn or a sacred song, and the offering of prayer. Yes, to restless, active boys it was sometimes a little "tedious." But it was "a matter of course." We knew of no other way of beginning and closing the day. We never dreamed of omitting it. We felt condemned when it seemed a "burden" to us. No, we were not very "good boys." I can only speak positively on this matter for myself. I was far from being in any sense "a good boy," rather the reverse. But I am bound to believe that I am a better man than I should otherwise have been, and that I owe more than pen can record or tongue can tell to this faithful home training in the recognition of everyday obligation to God. The reality of a just and holy God, his actual presence always and everywhere, the solemn fact of personal responsibility to him for what we are and for what we do – these are the great verities in which we should train our children, and all this from their early childhood.

But one aspect of this religious truth was not sufficiently emphasized in that earnest and faithful home. It was no doubt by father and mother taken for granted, but that was not enough.[2] Religion and everyday life were not so interwoven as to make *all life*, secular and sacred, really religious. We were taught to be

2. Hand annotations in the Vincent papers at Bridwell Library indicate that *Northwestern Christian Advocate* misprinted the opening sentences of this paragraph as follows: "But one aspect of this religious truth was not sufficiently emphasized in that earnest and no doubt by father and mother taken for faithful home. It was no doubt by father and mother taken for granted, but that was not enough."

sure to carry our religion into everything and every place, but the religion we attempted to carry was something separate and apart from life. We must do our duty but we were not to account ourselves as really in a religious service to God when we were working with our hands at some task, as when we were kneeling in prayer or sitting "under the droppings of the sanctuary" as the fathers stated it. We did not realize that all work and all play of the right type were but parts of religious life, that the ruling motive is the main thing, that life in society, that recreation, that business in all its legitimate forms are so many divinely ordained opportunities for the development of personal character and for the building up of a permanent civilization.

We are not in this world, as Christians, to get well out of it as soon as possible. The principal thing is not heaven, nor is it personal "safety." The world is not a "wilderness" through which we journey. The main aim is not to reach "Canaan." The "end" of life is not the best part of life. We are here to develop character in God's way and after the divine ideals, and in harmony with the laws of character-building which God through Christ has revealed to us. We are in this world to aid in the development of a wise, strong, and positive civilization, so that our successors may have larger opportunity for making the world and the race stronger and wiser and better.

A little later on we moved to Lewisburg, where father went into the mercantile business, but he did not succeed to his liking and later (in 1852) moved to Erie, Pa., where he became a member of the firm of Vincent, Himrod & Co. – the principal member of the firm being Mr. B. B. Vincent, a cousin of my father and the father of the Right Rev. Boyd Vincent, now a bishop of the Protestant Episcopal Church.[3]

My father some years after this moved to Chicago, where he took charge of the Chicago branch of the Erie firm. He resided in Chicago the rest of his life. For years he was a victim of paralysis – "trembling palsy" it was called. He suffered greatly but was at last released. Little did I think in my boyhood days (when to think of my father dying filled me with distress) that the time would ever come when to see him silent in death would be a source of comfort. He was a kind father, although in the days of his vigor we boys sometimes thought him severe. He was strict in government and made a violation of law a serious matter for the thoughtless or willful offender. He rarely resorted to corporal punishment, but when he did it meant something. The offender was not likely to forget either the penalty or the offense. And after the matter was finally settled, the full measure of punishment inflicted, his tenderness and kindness made us love him more than ever. In fact I often felt that his administration in the training of his children was in many respects an admirable concrete illustration of the fundamentals of theology – an insistence upon obedience, an enforcement of law, an illustration of justice in the infliction of penalty, the exercise of mercy, and the setting forth of the divine grace toward repenting offenders. Home ought always to be a kindergarten of theology. And it may, at the same time, be the brightest, jolliest place in all the world, a place where fun and play and wit and wisdom abide and abound. "Humor," says Douglas Jerrold, "is the harmony of

3. The Protestant Episcopal Church was founded in 1789 as the successor body to the Church of England in the American colonies. Today it is generally known by the shortened name, The Episcopal Church.

the heart."[4] And another sane man said, although his name was Sterne[5]: "I live in a constant endeavor to fence against the infirmities of ill-health, and other evils of life, by mirth. I am persuaded that every time a man smiles – but much more when he laughs – it adds something to this fragment of life."

4. English dramatist Douglas William Jerrold (1803-1857).
5. Anglican clergyman and novelist Laurence Sterne (1713-1768), author of *The Life and Opinions of Tristram Shandy, Gentleman.*

CHAPTER 7

# The Autobiography of Bishop Vincent

## Fourth Paper[1]

---

***April 27, 1910***

The neighborhood known in my childhood as "Chillisquaque," where the stone bridge crossed the creek by that name, was about two and a half miles below Lewisburg, on the east side of the west branch of the Susquehanna. It was a really lovely place in the days of which I now write. There was the old Montour Ridge, the stone bridge across the creek, with its graceful arches, the fine trees, the creek itself a pleasant stream of water in those days, the smooth road crossing the mill race and climbing the hill toward Northumberland, combined to make a charming picture on which my eyes often rested in my childhood. To me it was always beautiful.

### *The New Home*

I well remember the comfort we found in that house of our own after the long and fatiguing travel from Alabama. And I recall with keenest pleasure the evening when the new piano from Philadelphia was unboxed and set up in the parlor and our "Cousin

1. *Northwestern Christian Advocate*, Vol. 58, No. 17, page 12.

Elizabeth Brown," filled the house with what to me was delightful music. She was an interesting and attractive girl and an admirable pianist. Father was a good singer, and as we all had some taste for music, we had many a delightful evening of music, secular and sacred, in our new Northern home. We two boys (my brother Bethuel and myself) had a small carriage which father had bought for us in Philadelphia, and a good time we had with it on the ample lawn just below the house; and we passed happy hours in play and exploration and the many new kinds of "work" in which we were initiated. Bright and jolly days they were.

All who took part in the pleasures of those "first days in Chillisquaque," except my brother and myself, have long since gone to "the other world," and only the pleasure of "remembering" remains. Yes, there is more than that, for deeper and stronger than that are the gracious influences which those early and gracious ministries developed.

## *Early Education*

The beginnings of our formal education were in the old house at the foot of Montour. Father engaged a teacher or governess for us, a Miss Faries of Milton, who gave us lessons every day, and living in the home with us, was able to give us constant attention. The text-books are forgotten now. The teaching was inwrought into the texture of personality. The teacher herself has passed into the "other world." But those days of effort and acquisition, of blunders and reproof, of mother's solicitude and teacher's fidelity, have not all been wasted, but remain as silent influences in character, and to some extent have contributed to the benefit of the world. Nothing is lost. Well would it be for us if we might always weigh every passing opportunity and do the work of the moment with an eye to the far-reaching consequences.

And perhaps I shall find no better place in these pages of reminiscence than just here to make a plea for the home as the school of religious truth and that by the "object-lesson" method. "There is no place like home" for the right start in the process of education. There the first and most permanent impressions are made; and that through the living example of the people we know best and see oftenest. The real kindergarten of theology is the home. There all the great principles of religion and ethics may easily be taught in a series of effective object-lessons. And there above all other places the emphasis may easily be made, more easily and more early and more effectively, on *the one great factor* in education – the proper training of the WILL. That should be the first lesson and the fifth and the fiftieth. And home and only home has the best chance to make this part of education complete. This emphasis cannot be made too early. It cannot be insisted upon too frequently. It cannot be urged too strenuously. No theory of theology should be allowed to weaken conviction concerning it.

## *Religious Training*

It is reported that Daniel Webster was once asked this question: "Mr. Webster, what is the most solemn thought that ever entered your mind?" It is said that the distinguished statesman bowed his head reverently for a moment and then replied: "Gentlemen, the most serious thought that ever entered my mind is the fact of my personal responsibility to Almighty God." This great lesson of religious responsibility we must teach to our children, and we cannot begin this process of religious and theological training too early. When a child is old enough to learn the fact of his obligation to his parents, he is old enough to learn about both his obligation and theirs to the Supreme Creator and Ruler of the universe, "our Father who art in heaven."

My home was a kindergarten of religious and Church life. Possibly in some respects it was overstrict. But the fundamentals were set forth in the everyday teaching and domestic administration: God, law, gospel, ideals, personal responsibility, sin, redemption, the blessedness of heaven, the reality and the terrors of hell, the fact of a final judgment – all these were emphasized and insisted upon until everything else in life was to some extent overshadowed by them. I think I know all the terror and anxiety which a firm faith in these awful doctrines (as awful as the facts of everyday life) is bound to excite in the careful student of them.

No, I was not "a good boy." Rather the reverse (but this is not a "confessional"). I lived, for the earliest years of my life, in terror. When the Millerite excitement was "on" and a comet put in an appearance every night for weeks, and reports were made to me by schoolmates of the "second Advent" meetings in the "Christian" Church of the town, I used to be filled with anxiety which no "consolations of the gospel" that I knew anything about were able to alleviate.

### *Getting Ready for Life*

We live in stronger, wiser, nobler times. Let us thank God for that. The emphasis of wise Churchmen now is on the *present*. We are now urged by sane Christian leaders and teachers to live for "this life" – this life truly interpreted. We are as Christians to live for civilization, for better government, for a more thorough and symmetrical education, with a sense of responsibility for a better social order, for wiser education, having the spirit of self-sacrifice for the public good, and a vision of a Christian civilization here on earth and within the century we call our own. And we do all this work for the present by a vital, fervent faith in the spiritual truths and the Christian ideals which Christ has given to the world.

I take time and space in the beginning of my life story to make this fundamental emphasis because it is the recognition of this earth-and-time mission of the Church that makes the work of the Church "worth while" [sic] under the civilization of our day.

When these thoughts became verities to me, they gave a new significance to life. It is a delight to live under a system which provides three hundred and sixty-five holy days every year, and which gives a new sanctity and value to the holy Sabbath and the Church of Christ. Thus have Horace Bushnell[2], Robertson, some of the modern commentators on Swedenborg[3], with Professors Bowne, Fairbairn, and others opened to me a much larger and richer world of religious and spiritual verities than was within sight in my childhood.

Our own Mercein of New York had a glance at that realm, and an inner life that was quickened by it.[4] The little known and now forgotten Henry Hurd of New Jersey lived in its light, and walking with modern scientific men, rejoicing in their enriched and enlarged horizon, also "walked with God" every day, having sweet "fellowship with the Father and the Son." And it is a comfort and an inspiration to think of the increasing number of thoughtful, earnest, devout, growing men and women of our times who live "the life of the Spirit" and to whom the rich realm it represents

2. American Congregational minister and theologian Horace Bushnell (1802 – 1876) is mentioned numerous times in Vincent's narratives.
3. Swedish theologian Emanuel Swedenborg (1688 – 1772).
4. Thomas Fitz Randolph Mercain (1825-1856), MEC clergyman and writer, author of Natural Goodness (1854).

is as much "under law" and is as truly "scientific" and is all the while producing "phenomena" in the world psychological as the mysterious world of "matter" about which the "scientists" know and talk and write so much.

CHAPTER 8

# The Autobiography of Bishop Vincent

# Fifth Paper[1]

---

***May 4, 1910***

As a boy I did not have many boy friends. Perhaps the nearest and best whose friendship passed info my early manhood was William H. Armstrong of Lewisburg and later of Easton, Pa. – a lawyer of ability, son of one of the principal members of the Lewisburg Methodist Church and brother-in-law of Rev. John W. Elliott, whose colleague I became later on in the old Baltimore Conference. Armstrong was a sensible, cultivated, humorous, genuine, companionable fellow with whom between my fifteenth and twentieth year I spent many a pleasant hour. John Rhodes of Milton, the son of a retired and excellent Methodist, was another near and dear friend.

It has often been a problem in my mind as to why I had in my early years so few boy companions. I sometimes think it was because I in my early years never did have a wholesome and spontaneous boy life. I was to myself a problem. I began too early to think about the severe and gloomy side of religious life. The constant pressure upon the far-away and eternal future – the eschatological emphasis – the over-emphasis of the dark side of theology

1. *Northwestern Christian Advocate*, Vol. 58, No. 18, pages 14 and 32.

had a bad effect upon my personality, as it kept me all the while anxious about "death" and "final judgment," the "second coming" and all that. And the most unfortunate feature of this kind of anxiety is that it neither increases the sense of obligation nor does it make the religious life more attractive. It does excite alarm, developing selfish anxiety and cowardice and at the same time weakens one's sense of responsibility for a sane adjustment to the immediate conditions of one's life. It really tends to abnormality and to unreality, turning everyday life into a sort of monastic bondage and thus weakening individuality and destroying spontaneity.

It was this overemphasis of truths relating to the far future and the failure to see the value of the present life on its secular side as a true school of character that made my early life morbid and unreal.

It was the reading of Bushnell in his earliest volumes and of Robertson and of Canon Fremantle[2] in his "The World as the Subject of Redemption" that confirmed my conviction concerning the real significance of "the life that now is" as only a part of "the life that is to be." And these readings impressed me with the reality of "the reign of law" in all realms, so that one may frame a science of the world of spirit – a field of thought life and experience trustworthy and fascinating – more fascinating than any of the wonders that the physical world has to offer even to the devout student. And I may here say that modern, so-called "Christian Science" (possibly as unscientific as human speculation is ever likely to be) gains its hold for a time on the large class of people who believe that the realm of spirit, from the God who is Spirit must be under the control of forces and subject to a series of processes as truly scientific as are the phenomena and energies in what we

2. William Henry Fremantle (1831-1916).

call the realm of matter. There is a divine "science" in the realm of spiritual and religiously ethical life, as perfectly in harmony with "law" as anything we find in nature. And when we duly emphasize the freedom and responsibility of personality, the "reign of law" becomes as reasonable and as valuable when applied to spirit as when we recognize it in the fields of the material.

And this recognition gives a great advantage to the teachers of the spiritual life as they set forth the divine order according to which all things are carried on by the God of nature who is also the Father of spirits. As free he uses nature, and he makes us free that we may use nature in harmony with the laws he has established. So there is a science in the realm of matter and also in the world of spirit. And the two do most charmingly correspond. Parables flash out in the light of sun and stars, and all the fields of the divine creative activity are full of spiritual suggestions, and all the ways of man in every department of human life are images, correspondences of the mysterious and glorious kingdom of God.

Henry Drummond in his enlightening and quickening little volume, "Natural Law in the Spiritual World," has presented this subject in a most attractive fashion. There is a science of the personal spiritual life. And it is the humble and obedient follower of the Christ who is most likely to arrest the attention of the really teachable scientist. It was the earnest and spiritual Moody, who knew well the phenomena and laws of the Christian life, who appealed to the accomplished, elegant, and scientific Drummond, who was led by Moody into a new life of the spirit and was thus prepared to pen the little monograph to which I have referred.

And this is what the Church of this age most needs: Representatives of the laws of life in the spirit who also understand the laws of God in the material world. The demand of to-day is a sanctified and scientific scholarship. And the ministry of to-day needs a new interest in the fields of human learning, in the departments of the material and the social. And the new emphases on social science and the increasing enthusiasm in the cause of humanity, the conventions, the literature, the university chairs endowed, the elaborate courses of study, the popular interest in all reform movements – these give new hope and confidence to all followers of the Christ.

The problem of problems for the parents, pastors and so-called educators of this age is the right training of childhood and especially of adolescence in the relation of religion to life – to "this life." Here is the problem: How to put into everyday life – home life, school life, business life, and recreative life – the serious conviction concerning the reality of all life which, without making any one of these relations seem unreal and artificial will develop intelligent conscientiousness, personal purpose and reverent faith in the true type of Church life, and make religion a matter of everyday reality. Sabbath must not be made a burden but it must be used as an opportunity (pleasurable within certain lines of restraint) for the emphasis of *personal obligation to God* in all the relations and for all the activities of life.

This large question cannot be tossed aside with a scornful or even frivolous reference to the "old Puritanic regime." No man as father, no woman as mother in our age, with the peculiar perils of our civilization can afford to speak lightly of this problem of problems. It should be discussed in the pulpit, and well for the pew if the parsonage can be thought of as an illustration of the most earnest things the pulpit can say on the subject. Church life that does not act upon and influence home life can be of little value to anybody. Home life that does not create reverence for and interest in Church life loses one half of its opportunity. An inconsistent parsonage has to be dumb where its voice is most needed.

If the reader happens to wonder why the writer of these pages has so much to say concerning his home training and especially because it appears to have been to some extent morbid in the tone and tendency of it, he may say that it would be impossible to understand many things in his life without this word of explanation. The failure to make secular life as secular life *sacred* is to draw a line of demarcation which the Word of God does not draw and to establish two standards of life, one for religious people and another for the non-professing. And this the Word of God does not do. We are to eat, to drink, to work, to think, for the glory of God whose we are and whom we serve. This emphasis on secular life demands increased attention to give it religious value that as followers of Christ we may be in all things and in all services truly the Lord's.

**CHAPTER 9**

# The Autobiography of Bishop Vincent

## Sixth Paper[1]

---

***May 18, 1910***

I attended school all through my early youth. For a time, when we first came from Alabama, we had a governess in the home – a Miss Faries from Milton. There was a room in which she gave us our daily instruction in reading, spelling, writing, arithmetic, and deportment. She tried to teach us how to read and write and to "speak properly" and to "be good" – as good as two such youngsters could be with their restlessness and love of fun, and early schooling in the doctrine of "total depravity." Miss Faries held us to our work with fidelity, and while under the circumstances we could not always be enthusiastically "fond of her," we were profited by her fidelity. What can children know about what is best for them? To be popular with one's pupils is not always a good sign. It is vastly better for a teacher to look a long way ahead and teach with an eye to power and achievement and appreciation in the far-away future than to covet for the present the smiles and soft words of complacent pupils who boast behind the teacher's back of the "easy time" and the successful "dodges" that are possible though his laxity in recitation room and "study."

1. *Northwestern Christian Advocate*, Vol. 58, No. 20, pages 14 and 32.

To train a pupil in noble ideals and the development of will power [sic] is the mission of the true teacher. And success in that is better than showers of smiles and benedictions in the present.

Later on I attended school in the Milton Academy and afterward in the Chillisquaque country schoolhouse, and still later in Lewisburg, first in an old schoolhouse near the bridge that crossed the west branch and then in the academy where a cultivated and vivacious Irishman taught, Pollock by name, an energetic, impulsive fellow, really a scholar, a bundle of nerves, and on the whole (as I was able in those early years to judge him) a skillful and successful teacher. Then for a time we had one Robinson, nearsighted, who looked at you through his strong spectacles and made you feel that he was looking through *you* at the same time. A little before I was under the care of Robinson I had a teacher in the Chillisquaque schoolhouse by the name of Starke – a positive and overstrict teacher of the old, old times who wielded the rod and sometimes applied it, and who had the rare gift of expectorating tobacco juice from almost any part of the schoolhouse to the stove hearth, with an accuracy which excited the admiration of those of his pupils who had the temerity to look away from their books in order to watch his aim while they wondered at this skill.

And in that same old country schoolhouse we were for a winter under the care of a clear-headed, calm, quiet Quaker in drab, with a will in him. His name was Jesse Broomall, a sincere, simple-hearted, self-controlled man. I remember his first speech to us at the opening session when he announced the "only rule" he thought necessary for his government and our own. He dwelt for some time on the value of the rule he intended to announce. Having won our close attention and excited our curiosity to the highest pitch, he said: "The one rule, the wonder-working rule on which I shall base my administration is this, 'Mind your own business.'" I think I never knew him to lose his temper. And to-day after, well, let me say, more than sixty-six years, the memory of Jesse Broomall is to me a source of genuine pleasure. I do not think that he "thee'd" and "thou'd" like an old-time "Friend," but he left on my mind an impression that is to this day a source of pleasure, and as I recall him I seem to hear someone say, "There is a man, and a man to be trusted and respected." And I must add that when a personality can leave that impression on a boy's mind his influence as a teacher is significant and, as we say, "quite worth while."

The last group of teachers I became acquainted with was "the faculty" of the Newark (N.J.) Wesleyan Institute in Newark, N.J. While serving "under the elder" as assistant or "junior" preacher on the Newark City Mission in 1852, I became a student in the institute. There I came under the influence of Principal Chase, Professor Starr, and Professor Hale, and there and then (1852) I formed the acquaintance of the best of all my friends, the Rev. Dr. George H. Whitney, then a student, and registrar of the institution. I have never had a nearer nor a dearer friend outside of my own immediate family than George H. Whitney. We became at once "bosom friends" and have enjoyed the closest fellowship for these fifty-eight years. He is the incarnation of fidelity and uprightness in all the relations of life, and no man lives who more perfectly represents purity and honor. A mysterious providence has required him to suffer the most acute pain, but through all he has been a marvel of patience and submission to the will of God.

Among the most useful of my boyhood teachers were the "traveling preachers" who as our "pastors" under the old "circuit system" came from time to time to be our guests. The very memory of those chosen spirits is to-day a benediction. I am afraid to attempt to enroll their names lest one or more of the best of them be forgotten in the haste of writing. Who can forget the humorous and whole-souled John J. Pearce[2], and eloquent withal? The dignified and wise John A. Gere[3], a born bishop although never elected to that office; the vivacious and eloquent Benjamin Hamlin, and that other Benjamin, the sweet-spirited and heavenly-minded Benjamin Crever[4]; the loving and faithful pastor with a charming lisp in his speech, Thomas Taneyhill[5]; and Father Ewing, and Philip B. Reese, and John Elliott, and John Bear, and – but I must stop with the list incomplete.

What pastors they were, and what preachers! How firmly they believed the gospel and faithfully they preached it! Many of them were really eloquent. Some of them, although not great scholars from the schools, were men of prayer and men of power and specialists in the Book of books and in the wonderful mission of leading men to Christ. Their visits in farmhouses as they traveled the circuits were a benediction, and their fidelity in reproof and counsel – well, the simple memory of them is a silent rebuke to us in these days. The Methodist preachers of that day represented a great idea, an emphasis and a *life*. They carried books of theology in their saddlebags and handed stimulating tracts in person to saint and sinner, accompanying the gift with a word spoken in tones so tender that many a sinner was awakened, many a saint confirmed in his faith, and many a sorrow-smitten soul comforted.

2. Rev. John J. Pearce (1826-1912) was a minister in the Baltimore Conference of the Methodist Episcopal Church. He served one term in Congress, 1854-1856.
3. Rev. John A. Gere (1799-1874) preached under MEC appointments 48 years and also served as conference Sunday school agent.
4. Rev. Benjamin Heck Creaver, D.D. (1817-1890) was a Baltimore Conference Methodist minister who founded a private school in Milton, Pennsylvania. He was also one of the founders of Williamsport Dickinson Seminary, which opened in 1848 in Williamsport, Pennsylvania.
5. Rev. Thomas Taneyhill (1803-1904) entered the ministry in 1828. He served as an Elder in the Baltimore Conference of the Methodist Episcopal Church.

In many parts of our work, we still need the "circuit system." Its educating value to the preachers themselves cannot be overstated. The itinerating process is most valuable as it gives a young man a wider knowledge of our American civilization, and its advantage to families otherwise sure to be neglected, renders the abandonment of it little short of a crime. The "traveling preacher" was never needed so much as now, especially with the incoming of so many thousands of immigrants who, scattered in humble homes of their own and in neighborhoods where they have no chance to hear their own preachers, would welcome cordially the visits of honest, earnest, evangelistic circuit riders of the old type.

Methodism is in danger of neglecting the country to-day. What if the people coming in *are* foreigners? They all the more need the itinerant Methodist preacher with his saddlebags full of evangelistic and patriotic tracts to open the eyes of the newcomers to the distinguishing features of our civilization; to the fact of our freedom being a product of a pure and aggressive religious faith; to the demands in our country for a sense of personal independence and a sense of individual responsibility; to the necessity and inestimable value of the public school; to the fact that we offer absolute freedom to every man to think and act for himself and hence the necessity of education and of education in the public school.

Patriotism is the basis of the religion needed in America. This country is God's gift to the race. Personal freedom from all tyranny monarchical, governmental, ecclesiastical is absolutely necessary to patriotism. First God and then the nation and the Church. Reverence and love for and loyalty to the nation is the first duty to God. To love the flag and not the nation is disloyalty. And to love the Church more than the nation is another form of disloyalty. The

Church that places itself above the nation is a disloyal organization and has no claim on a really loyal American citizen.

The test of a religious system is its relation to the divine principles on which God has established the government under which a man lives. It may be a human and tyrannical government. Then God did not establish it. It may limit man's right to think for himself in his search for truth that shall guarantee the man's highest and noblest development as a man. God never so limits man. No Church has a right to do it. No man is bound to obey any regulation of any Church that interferes with his personal obligation to God and man. The sooner a man finds this out the better for the man, the nation, and the Church.

There is really room to-day to cover the territory of our annual conferences with an added "circuit" system, and to reproduce the old aggressive evangelistic policy, and that without in any serious way interfering with the work in "stations," which is now carried on by our preachers. We are neglecting the country and the smaller villages which under the old itinerant system made possible our success in the larger places to-day.

CHAPTER 10

# The Autobiography of Bishop Vincent

## Seventh Paper[1]

***May 25, 1910***

Although my grandfather Vincent was a descendant of an old Huguenotic family which in the beginning was Calvinistic, he became what was called "liberal" in his day, largely through the influence of the representatives of the Unitarian community in Northumberland, who occasionally visited and preached in Milton, and were the guests of my grandfather. He sympathized with their broader views. The Calvinism of the Presbyterians of that early day was either more pronounced or less understood than now and the Unitarian protest and corresponding platform were more acceptable to the people who accounted Calvinism "too rigid" and who had little or no sympathy with the so-called "evangelical theology."

Dr. Priestly, who had been exiled from England for his Unitarian "heresies" (as they were termed), had settled in Northumberland and quite a group of that sect gathered about him, and wherever they could they preached their views and protested against the rigidities of the old-time, "orthodox theology."[2] My

1. *Northwestern Christian Advocate,* Vol. 58, No. 21, pages 10 and 27.
2. Dr. Joseph Priestley (1733-1804), English scientist and Unitarian leader.

grandfather's blood was Huguenotic, his theologic views were possibly confused, his sympathies were naturally with the more "liberal" even the "heterodox" interpreters of the Christian faith. He was a prominent citizen, a man of unusual intelligence and influence, the postmaster of the town, the proprietor of the principal hotel, and as he always entertained the preachers from Northumberland, and as Unitarianism was a most emphatic protest against the extreme Calvinism of that day, my grandfather became interested in both the emphasis of the Northumberland preachers and the emphatic protest of the orthodox Presbyterians. Although his blood was Huguenotic his sympathies were with the so-called "liberals" in theology. The extreme views of old-time Calvinism must always be taken into account when we talk about or seek to understand the more "liberal" thinkers of a century ago. The protest of the so-called "skeptics" was a protest against an "orthodox" view which very few people in any evangelical Church hold to-day. And the term "orthodox" to-day means an entirely different thing from what the term implied even in my boyhood.

And again, in our estimate of religious doctrine we have come to put the chief emphasis not on dogma but on the personal surrender to one's idea of truth. A minimum of "orthodoxy" with a maximum of sincerity will be more useful to one's neighbors than all the truth in the world accepted intellectually merely as a creed and ignored in one's heart, life, and conduct. My mother, who knew little about theology as a formal statement of truth, but whose heart and will were fully surrendered to the truth she did hold, was a most effective factor in the training of her children and the influencing of her neighbors. Theology was taught in the house, and perhaps well taught, but the power in it was to be found in the personal experience, the consistent life, and the fervent prayers of the sweet woman we called "mother." The

Church to-day most needs this element in our home life and that will guarantee inevitably: vital faith, clear and positive experience, wise silence, judicious speech, a will surrendered to God, and the art of leaving all problems – personal and domestic – to the infinite wisdom, the infinite love, the perfect will of God

The subject of "holiness" as accentuated by Mr. Wesley was often discussed in our house, and while my mother never professed to have "attained" or "experienced" it, my father often said that if anyone ever had attained it certainly mother had. The intimation of such a thing in her presence would have shocked her, for she was so timid, modest, and retiring, so filled with a sense of her own unworthiness, that she could not listen to any word of praise. She was a most godly woman. She has been in "that other world" for more than fifty-five years. But the simple memory of her is an inspiration and a benediction.

It is a pity to turn "holiness" into a "doctrine" to be discussed and defined and defended. There is only one way to treat the whole subject: *Live* it. Don't talk much about it. Don't argue about it. It is an inexpressibly unfortunate thing to drag such a question into the realm of polemics. Let us simply aim to be surrendered to God – body, soul, spirit – every day, everywhere, and in everything – in business, at meals, at work, in society, in recreation, in politics, in study, in travel, going to sleep with the consciousness of God's presence and waking to look into the smiling face of "Our Father" – our Mother-Father – which God is. One word represents the whole subject of religion as applied to personal experience expressed in one word, *love* – for God, for man, for the world of nature we live in, for the world of grace we are new-born into, for the Church – all branches of it, for humanity at large, giving to it as individuals the largest sympathy, and the most sane and practical service. We are everywhere to practice *love;* at home when things "go wrong," and everywhere and always.

But my history is turning into exhortation and preaching. Well, with such a concrete illustration as the memory of my mother brings before me, preaching and exhortation and thanksgiving are spontaneous. Where such plants grow and such flowers bloom the air will be "laden with fragrance."

While I am writing of my mother let me record these few facts about her: She was brought up a Lutheran, became a Methodist in Alabama, was the intimate friend in Tuscaloosa, Ala., of Mrs. David Scott, and Mrs. Collier, became interested in the most earnest type of the spiritual life as represented at that time by intelligent and consecrated people. And thus our house became a center of religious and Church life, Catholic in spirit and loyal to the fundamentals of what used to be called "orthodoxy." But unkind words concerning other denominations were never heard in the home of my childhood. The children were trained to the double emphasis: the Church with an aim at earnest, practical, spiritual life and as one – one "Holy Catholic Church – the communion of saints" embracing all believers in Jesus Christ however they may differ on many points of dogma and on forms of Church government and worship.

An emphasis on the two aspects of Church life is important – the Church as Denominational and as Catholic. We are all one, if we believe in (so as to truly follow) the Lord Jesus Christ. We, by this recognition of the fundamental aim of Christianity keep as our ideal character the "*One* above all others" always before our thought. Our keynote is *Christ* and *Christ* alone. We may differ on many points concerning him and concerning his teaching. Therefore, the denominational opportunity to express and emphasize and to experiment with our respective theories about him. Any outward unity that compels the suppression of any theory concerning him, his offices, his requirements must work harm by suppression either of some great truth or some helpful experiment with an emphasis on some radical truth. Hence the incalculable value of denominational subdivision in order to the scientific experimentation on the individual and on society, that later on there may be certainty and finally a much more valuable and permanent unity.

It is this one feature of Church life in my home life which I thus desire and seek to emphasize: The denominational contribution to the really Catholic unity – a unity of intelligent, positive, thoughtful, earnest, individuals who "think for themselves" who choose "platforms" of theory and interpretation of the divine revelation and in an "experiment station" or colony of their own "try on" their hypotheses, test them on society, and thus contribute to the generation following the results of these earnest, practical, unselfish experiments with hypotheses, policies, and interpretations of the revelation of God – a revelation in a Book and that other revelation in a series of providential leadings of individuals and social groups and great ecclesiastical organizations, that out of all these human-divine processes may come the education and uplift, the enrichment, and the largest possible development of the race.

Therefore, the importance of denominational loyalty – loyalty to an emphasis and an organization and a policy. It need never interfere with loyalty to the family or to nation or to the Holy Catholic Church as embracing all sincere and devout followers of Jesus Christ. I always recite the Apostles' Creed omitting the semicolon and supplying the dash where the believer declares, "I believe in the Holy Ghost; the Holy Catholic Church – the communion of saints." And that is a good definition of the Holy Catholic Church.

## CHAPTER 11

# The Autobiography of Bishop Vincent

# Eighth Paper[1]

*June 1, 1910*

I began to preach and to teach before I was seven years of age – long before that, for I used to gather the little negroes on our place and neighborhood in Tuscaloosa to deliver sermons to them. Preaching was all the teaching they expected, and I was better qualified to proclaim and exhort than to edify by any sane pedagogic process. My little hymn book in one hand and a rod in the other, I was fully prepared to keep order and impart instruction.

I loved to teach and to preach from the earliest remembered period of my life. And, after all, preaching is teaching where it deals with truth and where it is skillful enough to excite interest, hold attention, and persuade people to think about the truth the preacher presents and to ask questions that they may the better understand the message the preacher attempts to deliver. Preaching is really teaching where it is *really* preaching. Very often preaching is simply the stirring of the people to feel an interest in a subject.

1. *Northwestern Christian Advocate,* Vol. 58, No. 22, pages 7 and 31.

I am afraid, however, that all the preaching and teaching I did in those earlier years was simply an attempt to reproduce the outward processes of pulpit discourse and public worship – to make gestures, "talk loud," imitate the preacher's manner, and carry through the "order of public service" from the announcement of the first hymn to the benediction. The boy-preacher cared very little about *what* he said to the child-congregation. The main thing was to "go through the motions." That was the "alpha" and the "omega" of these infantile ecclesiastical attempts.

But when I was fifteen years old I did, one summer, teach a regular school in the old Chillisquaque schoolhouse. And that was not "play" but an honest attempt to teach a regular school in the very schoolhouse in which the summer before I had been a pupil. And I think I may say that it was not wholly a failure. I was thoroughly in earnest and tried "to do a good job." I had probably about thirty children from the neighborhood. They were all younger than myself. I knew what I wanted to do. I was really in earnest. I made sure of "good order." I gave tasks to be studied at home by the pupils. In school I tested them to see what work they had done, and I kept a record of their work and of mine. I had very little "chastising" to do. I liked the youngsters and I think the most of them liked me. I enjoyed the experience and decided, from the "success" I had, to do some more of the same kind of work. The next summer I taught a school at Watsontown, four or five miles above Milton, near the Susquehanna River and not far from the old Warrior Run Presbyterian Church – a Presbyterian Church which most of the Vincents of that vicinity attended. I never heard much said about my school experience there, but I think it was a partial success. I know it gave me some experience and made me think that I had hidden away in me somewhere a measure of pedagogic ability, although I am afraid that at that time I was not familiar with the word "pedagogy."

It happened a little while after this that when I was in Milton clerking in my cousin John H. Raser's drug store, a traveling teacher of geography ("Singing Geography" as it was called) happened to organize a class in Milton and I joined it. As I was familiar with the facts of geography and had a taste for music and a tolerably good voice I mastered the art of teaching on the simultaneous method and became quite an expert in it. I conceived the idea of doing the same kind of work on my own account.

My father at first disapproved but finally consented, gave me the money to buy a set of "Pelton's Outline Maps" (thirty dollars it was, I think) and I went into the business. The plan was novel, and proved a success in creating enthusiasm, utilizing the child's fondness for simultaneous and musical exercises and making numberless repetitions easily possible, fixing numberless names in the memory and connecting by the use of outline maps the location and the name so that it was impossible to forget either. I taught the system for some months, father permitting me to experiment with the method on condition that I remained near home. I taught classes in Selinsgrove, New Berlin, Lewistown, and M'Veytown[2].

Wherever I went I found friends of my father. I attended our Church in every community where I taught and found many friends who were true and helpful to me. The field of my work was within our own (the Baltimore) annual conference, and all the preachers and many of the laymen knew my father and mother, so that I ran no risk from wrong companions, always attended Church and Sunday School, and all my associations were with our own denominational representatives.

2. McVeytown, Pennsylvania, in Mifflin County.

At the close of my term (with my class in singing geography in M'Veytown) the board of the public school asked me to take charge of the old academy, which I did. I remained for some time in dear old M'Veytown, where I was given a license as a "local preacher" by the quarterly conference. Brother Taneyhill, who had years before been preacher in charge of the circuit on the West Branch where our family lived, was the pastor who signed that license.

Among the happiest memories of my youth are of the days spent in M'Veytown. I boarded most of the time with a Mrs. Johnston, a widow who was kind and frank as a mother. I kept up a constant correspondence with my home. Among my first pupils, first in the "Palestine class" and then in the "academy" on the hill were some of the brightest and most interesting young people I have ever known, but a few months ago I visited the dear old place, was cordially welcomed by the pupils of other years – old men and women now – and preaching on Sunday morning in the Presbyterian Church and in the evening in the Methodist Church – the two congregations uniting in both services – had the pleasure of grasping the hands of old friends and recalling the years when as a mere boy I began to preach the gospel. In the afternoon of that Sunday, I went to the cemetery to find the graves of several of my most dearly loved pupils. I visited the upper room of the old academy where I taught. And it was a rare honor and opportunity in the evening of the Sunday to review before a large congregation the years of my stay among them and to tell the story of "Chautauqua," some of the features of which I had already anticipated in those long-ago years.[3]

3. This is the first reference to the Chautauqua Institution in Vincent's autobiography.

What a firm hold my mother had on me in those early years at the beginning of my "public life"! What letters she used to write me, full of counsel and affection, never forgetting to remind me how constantly I was in her thoughts and in her prayers, and how at the family altar "the absent boy is constantly remembered."

Was I such a "good boy" in those days of adolescence? Certainly not. I was a sensitive, self-centered, morbid boy. I had lofty ideals and a weak will. I dreamed and desired and decided and easily relapsed into old and accustomed moods. I lacked a certain type of boy-life which a college course just at that time would have secured to me. I was much of the time thinking about the coming of death, the awful judgment, the terrors of hell, the folly of "loving to play," the importance of "meditation" and "self-denial" and "seasons of prayer." To me some things in life were "secular" and other things were "sacred" and I "took" to the "secular" rather than to the "sacred" and no one told me what I did not learn until long afterward, that "all things" may be made sacred – play, study, society, fun, travel, business, etc.

It is just at this point I am compelled to criticize [sic] the home laxity that allowed me to omit the collegiate training as an essential part of my preparation for the ministry. For every reason a minister of the gospel in these days should be a college graduate. Perhaps the men who feel this the most keenly are the men with ideals who have been led or allowed to enter the active ministry without this preparatory training. The minister must know. He must know how and what to read, how to think, how to tell what he knows, how to look at every field of truth from more than one point of view. He should know how the thinkers of the ages, and especially of this age, have looked into the great problems of life – personal, domestic, social, political, national, universal. He should be able to appreciate the relative values of the fields of human learning.

But why attempt to catalogue the contents of the vast realm with which every preacher of the gospel as a pastor and a teacher and a leader in the civilization to which he belongs should be familiar?

CHAPTER 12

# The Autobiography of Bishop Vincent

# Ninth Paper[1]

---

*June 8, 1910*

It is a good thing to educate children with the constant forelook on mature life. A child well trained up, as the book puts it, must be held under control and with a wise measure of restraint, and at the same time must look forward, under parental guidance, to the coming years of responsibility, maturity, and large opportunity. It is an aid to the present acceptance of authority, to have before one and in constant anticipation the years of personal freedom and privilege yet to come; and to be taught that the discipline and limitations of to-day are a preparation for the liberty and larger privileges of to-morrow. And it is the intelligent, serious, sane teaching of religious truth and self-restraint during the early years that makes the well-controlled child the self-controlled man. And all this is equally possible in town and country.

But there must be especial care in the country to make the home as strict, as careful of the social proprieties as though one's house stood on a street or avenue of the city. It does not take many books to make a good library. Parents may be as critical and careful of a

1. *Northwestern Christian Advocate,* Vol. 58, No. 23, page 7.

child's manners in a solitary farmhouse as on a crowded avenue. Good grammar is as much "at home" and sounds as well in the farmhouse as in the palace. And is every bit as important. And in both places a good dictionary within easy reach, and the habit of consulting it frequently, in order to train children (and adults as well) in accuracy, will soon put on the tongue and in the voice of the farmer's boy the correctness and grace one expects to find in the parlor of the college or university president.

In one of my early pastorates in Illinois I knew a mother and her sons (and a daughter as well) who had formed the habit of reading the best literature and of turning home into school. They read a great deal of the best literature, under the evening lamp. And they talked about what they read. And soon the boys began to write for the press, and all went to college. And the boys gained reputation in literary, and later in political, circles; and largely because the mother believed in home training in the best and noblest things in life. Home is the best school. Let the press say it over and over again. Let the pulpit proclaim it. Let the schoolhouse echo and reecho with it. Let our intelligent farmers and all fathers and mothers everywhere experiment in this direction.

What has this to do with the task I have before me in these autobiographic pages? I may say, Everything. I thus pay tribute to a faithful father in whose library before I was born were the best books of his times: the then popular "Americana Encyclopedia," Pitkin's "Civil and Political History of the United States," Rollin's "Ancient History," Shakespeare, Gibbon's "Rome," "Paradise Lost," not to mention the wide field of poetry and the richer field of theology as represented by the leading Methodist writers, Wesley and Fletcher and Adam Clark, together with biographies of the devout representatives, not only of Methodism, but of the whole Christian world. Our weekly Church paper came to the house regularly, the Sunday School literature from not only our own but from the American Sunday School Union publishing house. And in addition to these standards, we had much of the then current literature of the so-called "higher life."

As I have already said, the atmosphere of the home of my childhood was thoroughly catholic in spirit. It was as loyal to the Methodists as John Wesley ever was, but it recognized the spirit of Methodism according to Wesley's idea wherever it appeared.

Having paid this tribute to the administration of my firm and, as I sometimes thought, over-strict, father, since this is my own autobiography, I may be permitted to say that my early life was restricted and often depressed by religious teachings in which personal "safety" and personal "religious happiness" were too commonly and strongly emphasized. I really lived under the "reign of fear" – a fear of God which was not the reverent love which that term embraces as used in the Bible, but a fear that was often, very often, "terror." I was always looking for the "day of judgment," for the "final account," and I constantly lived in anxiety lest "the end of the world" might be very near, as some of the preachers declared. I dreaded thunderstorms. I was afraid of death. I knew I was a "great sinner." Most of the time I was sure that if I should die the only place for me would be a place of the very "blackness of darkness." Once in a while I did have a flash of hope and again I became indifferent and then despondent. I was never really jubilant in my religious faith – as a youth – nor later, at least to any degree comparable to the enthusiastic and triumphant testimonies one often listened to in a love feast. I was prepared to defend the severe doctrines of the orthodox faith, and I was afraid of any theology that lowered the standards of the spiritual life as taught by the fathers or that made the way to heaven too easy. Certain texts of Scripture puzzled me when I looked on the future with the eyes of an optimist. Yes, I well know how narrow these views were. But I believed that it is a terrible thing to sin against God and that it is dangerous to make it appear "a light matter."

It is an evil thing to be too solicitous about one's own personal "safety." To be satisfied that I myself am "safe," to be myself "happy," to make that the main end of Church and religious life, must be a blunder. Is it not possible thus to foster the narrowest and most dangerous type of religious life? And may we not overemphasize certain theological truths and alarm people to the point where moral equilibrium is to such an extent disturbed as to render impossible the free and deliberate exercise of the will on which everything in the spiritual and moral life depends?

In certain types of old-time revivalism there was perhaps too much of what produced the effect of "coercion." Excitement may be so intense as to weaken and sometimes to destroy the personal freedom necessary to a genuine, permanent, character-making choice. And one ill effect is sure to follow, at least in many cases: A public profession made under undue pressure is soon, very soon, regretted, and often recalled, if not in form, in fact. And lifelong regrets are not the only results of this overpressure upon a free agent.

Of course, out of such devices may come certain permanent results, but none of any value that might not have been secured through a sane and normal process. No act is more momentous, no decision more important and sacred, than that by which a sincere soul chooses the way of the Lord in the sight of a witnessing world. And in urging and promoting this noble and divine end, let us avoid all questionable devices and everything that looks like superficiality.

## CHAPTER 13

# The Autobiography of Bishop Vincent

# Tenth Paper[1]

***June 15, 1910***

My first regular work as an itinerant minister was as junior preacher on the Luzerne Circuit of the old Baltimore Annual Conference. The preacher in charge of the circuit was John W. Elliott, a thoughtful, sensible, devout, and practical man, whose wife was the daughter of Mr. William Armstrong of Lewisburg, and her brother Henry (afterward a leading lawyer of Easton, Pa.) was my most intimate boy friend.

The Luzerne Circuit extended from a point several miles below the village of Conyngham to a charge several [miles] above While Haven on the Lehigh River. Among the Churches (or, as we called them, appointments) on the circuit were Hazleton, Weatherly, Beaver Meadows, and Janesville. There were several preaching places beside these. It was a four weeks' circuit, requiring that length of time to make one round in filling the list of services. That meant much travel. I had a good horse, saddled and bridled, a pair of saddlebags, good health, ambition, a lively imagination, a good deal of enthusiasm, on the whole a true motive, a small stock of sermon notes, a few very good books, cordial welcomes from a

1. *Northwestern Christian Advocate*, Vol. 58, No. 24, pages 7 and 30.

score of pleasant homes, frequent letters from a faithful father and an angel of a mother. I knew that every day at the home altar and in the place of secret prayer I was remembered before God.

As I review that part of my life, I wonder that I could even have entertained the thought of entering the ministry without a college preparation. But that was the custom in those days. Men without college training read law in a lawyer's office, passed examination, and were admitted to the bar. Men read medicine under the direction of a competent physician and became doctors. Men experienced religion, were on examination licensed as local preachers, traveled a circuit under the direction of a senior preacher, took a four years' course of study in theology, Church history, etc., practiced in pulpit and pastoral work under an older and experienced preacher, and became by vote of the annual conference, first deacons, and two years later, elders, being ordained to these orders by a bishop.

These examinations were conducted at the seat of the annual conference by men competent to judge of the proficiency and ability of the candidates. There have been, no doubt, many cases where the examination was superficial, especially where the candidate was known to be a really effective and successful preacher and pastor, building up his Churches, winning souls to Christ, attracting interested audiences, and so representing the great benevolent enterprises of the Church as to secure liberal collections in their behalf from the members of his Church and congregation.

As a rule, the tests applied to candidates for our ministry are strict and just. The system of the itinerancy has certain advantages as a process of training for the Christian ministry. It has promoted the most thorough training. And to-day many strong Congregational and Presbyterian and Protestant Episcopal pulpits are occupied by men educated in the old Methodist fashion by circuit or station *praxis*, the annual conference examination for four consecutive years, the fellowship frequently for this period with an associate and confidential friend either as senior preacher on the same circuit, as neighbor on an adjoining circuit or station, or as a frank, friendly, experienced presiding elder of the same district. And the intimacy fostered by the Methodist system between the preacher young and old and the most earnest and intelligent laymen, has been an educating factor well worthy of being taken into account when estimating the influences which tend to the development of pulpit and pastoral power in our Church. We are glad to report that the strenuous efforts of our more scholarly ministers, sustained by the efforts of our most earnest and progressive laymen have secured funds for building and endowing colleges, universities, and theological schools, so that every year our annual conferences are receiving a larger number of men into the ministry who come through both college and theological seminary.

It is, however, well to remember that God does call some men to places of largest influence in both state and Church who have not been prepared for that divinely appointed field by the processes of culture which the academicians have outlined. As a rule, these are the men who are most emphatic in their insistence upon the higher education. They know by bitter experience what it is to be hampered in the prosecution of a professional service by the consciousness of insufficient preparation. And it is the duty of all who are in authority to hold up the highest standards of preparation, and at the same time to recognize the hand of God in the exceptional cases, so that in all things we may be workers together with God.

It cannot be out of place or in any sense objectionably egotistic if on these pages, devoted to the story of my own life, I again refer to the lack I have here and everywhere lamented – my own failure to prepare for professional life by a course of college training. Partly through natural eagerness to be, before my time, in the field of active life; partly through the plausible but erroneous notion that God can do his best work, or that he chooses to do his best work through instruments whose feebleness may the more positively emphasize his power; partly because the rapidly developing Methodist movement tempted the leaders of it to lower the standards in order to secure the men in sufficient numbers to keep up the record of annual increase – like many others I *did* begin too early to exercise the ministerial functions. Of course, God's way is always best. But one may fail to wait long enough to find out just what God's way is, and himself anticipate and adopt a policy which the divine plan might greatly modify and improve. Lifelong limitations, unnecessary and burdensome, may result from the adoption of one's own scheme of life.

It is a good thing to *wait*. The best place to wait is in college. Waiting there may widen one's whole view of life, as it is bound to enrich it. A man eager to save souls will find scores of souls to save in every college. If he would begin to practice on folks that he may have skill in adaptation to individuals there is no place where folks are so much in need of example and influence and effort as on the college campus, in the recitation room, and in the intimacies and ambitions and ideals of the fraternities. Then a college and seminary graduate has much larger influence, to begin with, in any pastoral field, and a *prestige* in the pulpit when he rises to preach. He speaks with the authority which a reputation for scholarship guarantees, at least in the beginning of his labors in any place, and if he really be a student, the fact known in his congregation and the community will continue to give him an advantage while his ministry is earnest and practical. It is something to have the good name and wide repute of a great university or a strong college as a pulpit background.

My experience as assistant preacher on a large circuit was of great value to me. It was a kind of academic *praxis*, a ministerial seminar, bringing me into contact with so many, and so many different kinds of people – both town and country folks – and bringing us into mutual relations most favorable for the careful, thorough, conscientious, and both critical and sympathetic study of human nature.

And here let me say that every preacher should have some experience in preaching and pastoral work in the country. We find there two classes who need the pastor's influence and assistance: the American country youth who are soon to be in the city, and the immigrants who are settling on our farms and who need the counsel, sympathy, and personal influence of pronounced and educated Americans. We should, as I have elsewhere insisted, show them our interest in them and help them to understand the distinctive doctrines of the republic and the true American ideals.

The quiet and monotonous life of the country is either helpful or harmful, as it depresses or stimulates. Its very stillness may give us opportunity to read and think, or it may lull us into a state of stupor. There are country people who become like quiet, harmless, stupid, satisfied animals, eating, sleeping, working, waiting for something to turn up.

It is our business as Christian workers to imitate the fathers in the Church, looking up and looking after the newcomers, not neglecting the old settlers. We need a country circuit mission for the visitation of the farmhouses, the distribution of good literature, calls on the immigrants, bidding them with a friendly smile a welcome to America. We should look after their children and be, as Christians and Americans, as aggressive as Romanist priests are.

## CHAPTER 14

# The Autobiography of Bishop Vincent

# Eleventh Paper[1]

---

***June 22, 1910***

It was an interesting and profitable experience – that first year on a circuit, in the heart of the mountains, as a "junior preacher" and little more than a boy. My "senior" was John W. Elliott of the Baltimore Annual Conference, who had served on our home circuit and knew my parents well. He had married my sister's most intimate friend – Mary Armstrong, a gentle, pious, and refined girl from Lewisburg and from the Church in which I had practically been brought up. Mr. Elliott was a genuine, steady, thoughtful, consistent Christian man, and an excellent preacher. He was short in stature, had black eyes, black hair, was of dark complexion, thoroughly English and well Americanized.

As "junior preacher" I had no responsibility except to follow the directions of my "senior" – preach, visit, study, travel, think, pray, get well acquainted with folks, make friends, especially with the youngsters in the homes I visited, consult on all questions of administration with my senior, submit "cases" and "situations" to him, accept his decisions and sustain his administration as

1. *Northwestern Christian Advocate,* Vol. 58, No. 25, pages 10-11.

the "preacher in charge." And this relation is most helpful to the "young preacher" as it trains him to study human nature, and take lessons in real social life – now in the lovely homes of the so-called "best people" of the circuit, and now in the "humblest" (sometimes the cleanest, most cordial, most intelligent, and most inspiring) homes of the miners and mechanics and farmers belonging to the Church. Some of these (many of them) were from England, some from Wales, a few from old Ireland, while many of them were Americans, only weakened a bit by the American notion that as Americans they were better, wiser, and of course more "independent" than any other people on the face of the globe.

I found many good books on the shelves of humble homes, patience and submission to the order of divine providence, heard many a story of real life and of the "inner life" I might possibly not have heard in a very rich man's house; gained definite ideas concerning the workingman's sphere and experiences on the other side of the sea, and listened to many a pathetic story of separation, bereavement, struggle, aspiration, purpose, and of divine providences which made me love these genuine and so-called "humble people," and prepared me to appreciate their fixed attention as I talked my simple talks on Sunday that were called "sermons" and to which I think they listened with more sympathy and appreciation and prayers in my behalf because of the occasional pastoral visits and chats we had together in their humble homes.

Pastoral calls on an afternoon (where one has a "station") between three and six o'clock, covering certain streets and sections of the town or city, with honest words of counsel and comfort, will enable a pastor to "get around" so often every three or six months and will make a most interesting and "praiseworthy" report to the "official board" and to the "presiding elder," and these reports kept on record and duly announced by the "district superintendent" when a "preacher's character is passed" will sound well in the ear of the "brethren" and elicit a smile from an attentive bishop.

But the best fruits of all this pastoral fidelity are not to be found in the fields of "officialdom" and in the sessions of the annual conference, but in the softened hearts of the "folks" themselves; and the echo of them may be heard in the private prayers and thanksgivings of poor and sometimes afflicted or discouraged souls to whom the pastor's presence and handshake and smiles and words of both counsel and consolation are like visits from the angels of God.

I sometimes wonder if our people and the preachers of this period realize how much advantage to the spiritual life of the Church of fifty and more years ago the old circuit system was and how much we have lost in various ways by the abandonment of the system with its presiding elder's visitation, its less frequent "sermon," it's "senior" and "junior" preachers, with their "calls" which generally meant a "visit" for a night at a time, or a whole afternoon. Then there were the blessed "love feasts" – well, we do still have them with probably less of the old-time enthusiasm. And there was more of the social spirit then than now; fewer chances now for a good, old-fashioned chat with grandfather or the dearest of old-time grandmothers, whose stories of the "old preachers" and the "old quarterly meetings" were almost like a real revival for the preacher himself, who often on his way home from that little season of reminiscence asked God to spare the dear old sister or the sweet-spirited old grandfather until the Church of to-day has restored to it the cordiality, the freedom, the vital experiences of that old-fashioned Pentecost-like past.

I sometimes wonder if the young preachers of to-day realize how much they have lost in having been born so late. Some of them are shut up in little villages when they might have shared with some wise and spiritually-minded senior a field twenty or thirty miles in extent with ten or more little congregations under their care. Preaching the same sermon over and over is not always a bad thing to do. It is likely to lead to revision. It is likely to be enriched by the candid criticisms and suggestive questions of honest folks who know human nature to the core and have had richer experiences, perhaps, than the preacher himself, in the things of God. And how often is it the case that casual remarks and direct questions humbly propounded to the preacher open to him new fields of thought, new applications of a principle, new illustrations for use in the pulpit – illustrations for which "that eminent and eloquent city preacher" would gladly have given the fee he received for one of this latest and best lectures.

The death of my sister Ann Eliza and of my mother within three days left our home desolate. The former was called "sister" although only a cousin, the daughter of my mother's brother, who, when her father and mother died (before my birth) was "adopted" by my parents as their own child and was always called "daughter," and to me she was always "sister." It even seems strange to me now to record the fact that she was "cousin." Her own brother, Dr. John H. Raser, for years a leading citizen of Reading, Pa., was a man of exceptional ability, gentle, refined, scientific, and artistic in his tastes.

Ann Eliza Raser was a most unselfish, affectionate, and conscientious girl, devoted to my parents whom she always called "father" and "mother." Her early training was at the Moravian Seminary at Lititz in Lancaster County, Pennsylvania. She was humble, gentle, patient, and devout; about six years my senior. She was always dutiful, sympathetic, consistent, and faithful to every trust. I have never known a more amiable person. Her death, two days before that of my mother, was to us a sore affliction. But she died in triumph, having a perfect faith in Christ and an assurance of the life immortal.

I find it difficult to report the details of her departure. It was death that was not DEATH. Rather it was an entrance into the gates of eternal LIFE, and the room was radiant as with light from heaven. To us, in those days, after our long and faithful training in the reality of the eternal life, death seemed almost like a celestial messenger. The dear girl believed in the reality of heaven as certainly as we believe in "to-morrow," and to her it was really a glad TO-DAY. She sang, on her deathbed, very sweetly two or three of the old sacred songs we had been accustomed to sing at our family devotions especially at the Sabbath twilight service which we always held at home after the Sabbath evening meal.

At the time of my "sister's" death, mother, who was ill in another room, was brought at her urgent request into my "sister's" room. And then followed a scene too sacred for me to attempt to report – a parting full of love and hope and triumph. It was the consummation of a life of unselfishness and fidelity. The unspiritual worldling who cares little for the verities of the "inner" and the "other" life sees nothing in such a passage out of this world but an innocent and empty "fancy." To the believer in the divinity of the Christian religion it is far otherwise. As the dear girl breathed her last, mother exclaimed in a voice soft and sweet, "Hallelujah!" And as I recall that scene I involuntarily think of the apostle's exclamation, "O death! Where is thy sting? O grave! Where is thy victory?"[2]

The Sabbath that followed was a solemn day. In the parlor below lay the still form of our beloved sister; in the room above, between life and death, the best mother that ever lived.

2. I Corinthians 15:55, King James Version.

Very early on Monday morning (only a little after midnight) a special messenger came to my room from my mother, asking me to come to her, but asking me to be as quiet as possible so as not to disturb and alarm father. As I entered her room she said, "My son, I have sent for you to read some Scripture to me, to steady my mind. And I want you to pray with me. I want to retain my reason and I need the Word of God." She indicated certain passages which I read. As she closed her eyes, I kneeled in prayer. Then she thanked me and bade me go to bed again. Her physician heard her pray that night that God would preserve her reason that she night be able in her death to show her children and her neighbors how dying grace is given to the children of God. And her prayer was fully answered.

There was a time when I could not have reported this scene without going into the details of it. But I must not attempt that. Mother died in the full triumphs of the Christian faith. Her life was a testimony worth a score of deathbed declarations. But her words at the last, and her smiling face, and the looks of love she left us with – well, they can never be forgotten by those who stood by her side that winter day. Precious mother! What wealth of human love still remains for thee among the loyal few who still linger on this side of the "river" and of the "city" and of the "throne."

Soon after the funeral of my mother we prepared to leave the Susquehanna Valley for Erie where my father entered into business. I went to Newark, N. J., not having decided upon any plan for the future. Visiting for a few weeks relatives in Newark, I was invited to accept an appointment "under the elder" as the position is defined in the Methodist parlance. It was suggested that I might study in the Newark Wesleyan Institute and at the same time serve the "City Mission." I accepted the position. I was to assist Rev. Garner R. Snyder, who had charge of the mission, find my home among the best Methodist families of the city, preach on Sundays, and otherwise assist the "senior preacher" of the charge. So I studied and recited in the mornings, visited officially in the afternoons, occasionally preached in the evenings.

I am greatly indebted to my own dear relatives in Newark the Hartshorne family, for constant attention, wise ministries, genuine sympathy, and social opportunities during that experimental period of my New Jersey life. And there was the faithful "Sister Hill," long since gone to the better land, a most diligent and faithful servant of the Church in Newark and perhaps the most enterprising and faithful representative of the City Mission. My year of work in the Newark Wesleyan Institute was of great value to me. The president of the institution was Sidera Chase. He was succeeded by Professor Benedict Starr. The preceptress of the institute was Mrs. Mary F. Green. Her maiden name was Fiske. Mr. Green died leaving a son whose name was "John Green." This suggests an interesting biographical item. A friend of mine who knew him and his parents well says, "John was not a handsome fellow. He had a badly freckled face and was stout and uncouth." His mother married again and took a notion to change the boy's name. And she called him "John Fiske" after her own maiden name which was "Fiske." To-day her son as John Fiske, whose earthy career ended several years ago, is known and widely known and honored in the realm of literature. He was a lecturer on philosophy at Harvard; for a time a tutor there, and he wrote also extensively on scientific subjects.

In the spring of 1853 I became a member "on trial" of the New Jersey Conference, and was appointed to North Belleville (Franklin) which charge I served for two years. I boarded for a time with the family of Brother John K. Spear and then with Brother John S. Brown. I did greatly enjoy this my first regular "appointment" as a member of an annual conference. My quarters were small, fare good, treatment as kind as though I had been a member of the family, and the members of that little Church treated me with hospitality and generosity. I studied with a degree of faithfulness, preached short sermons, visited the people, gave special attention to the children and young people and did not neglect the old.

John Himrod Vincent (1798-1873) and Mary Raser Vincent (1803-1852), the parents of John Heyl Vincent.

*Courtesy of Bridwell Library Special Collections, SMU, Dallas, Texas.*

The Vincent home in Chillisquaque, Pennsylvania.

*Courtesy of Bridwell Library Special Collections, SMU, Dallas, Texas.*

Bench Street Methodist Episcopal Church Galena, Illinois, circa 1857-1877.

*Courtesy of Bridwell Library Special Collections, SMU, Dallas, Texas.*

Stereo card image of John H. Vincent seated in front of his tent at Chautauqua, circa 1878.

*Courtesy of Chautauqua Institution Archives, Chautauqua, New York.*

Old First Night observances in the Chautauqua Institution amphitheater, August 1900.

*Courtesy of Bridwell Library Special Collections, SMU, Dallas, Texas.*

John H. Vincent and Lewis Miller postcard image, 1899.

*Courtesy of Chautauqua Institution Archives, Chautauqua, New York.*

Bishop John H. Vincent Returning from Switzerland, 1902.

*Courtesy of Chautauqua Institution Archives, Chautauqua, New York.*

John Heyl Vincent and Sarah Elizabeth Dusenbury Vincent riding in a horseless carriage, circa 1904-1908.
*Courtesy of Bridwell Library Special Collections, SMU, Dallas, Texas.*

Jacon Riis, Theodore Roosevelt, and John H. Vincent at Higgins Hall, Chautauqua, August 11, 1905.

*Courtesy of Chautauqua Institution Archives, Chautauqua, New York.*

Bishop John H. Vincent speaking in front of the Hall of Christ (Aula Christi), Chautauqua Institution, circa 1909.
*Courtesy of Bridwell Library Special Collections, SMU, Dallas, Texas.*

Bishop John H. Vincent and Jane Addams, circa 1915.
*Courtesy of Chautauqua Institution Archives, Chautauqua, New York.*

CHAPTER 15

# The Autobiography of Bishop Vincent

## Twelfth Paper[1]

*June 29, 1910*

I now take up the story of the most interesting and in some respects the most important quadrennium of my first twenty-four years of life. It embraces my first and formal four years of pastoral life. I had been a local preacher. I had served for one year as assistant pastor on a country circuit in the heart of Pennsylvania, and I had been for one year junior preacher on a city mission in New Jersey. Now I became a "preacher on trial" and in charge of a little Church of my own, in the heart of the country, but near to the great city of New York and still nearer to the growing city of Newark, and "no mean city" was Newark even sixty years ago. My little Church was within easy reach of the very center of our best civilization, and the choice could be easily made between the busy life of Broad Street in Newark, Broadway, New York, or the quiet, well-shaded, pleasant rural paths of North Belleville; and one could easily walk from the humble church in the center of that quiet neighborhood to the very heart of the growing and ambitious city by the Passaic. And in this walk to Newark from the little church in Franklin (as North Belleville was

1. *Northwestern Christian Advocate,* Vol. 58, No. 26, pages 10-11 and 32.

sometimes called), one could stroll for half the distance by the side of the Passaic River, and, passing one of the most beautiful cemeteries of the continent, enter into the heart of the stirring, growing city of Newark.

But in spite of the opportunity to travel I found most pleasure in my quiet study, among my friendly parishioners; now having a most inspiring debate with the aggressive, thoughtful, earnest John Rusby; now a humorous tilt with odd old Aunt Polly Spear; now a tender and inspiring season of conversation with the spiritually-minded and heaven-bound Phebe Furlong; then – but I cannot call the roll of the dear old friends of 1853-55. Most of them are in heaven now: the Browns and the Simpsons, and the Rutans, and the Spears, and the Bowmans, and all the rest; in heaven, where Henry Hurd is, about whom they talked so much when I first went to North Belleville that I began to wonder if I had any chance to "hoe a row" or "make a mark" or get a "hearing" where "Hurd" was on everybody's tongue, his picture on everybody's wall, and a marvelous love for him in everybody's heart. So I found out where the wonderful Hurd was, and I wrote to him, and sent him a check, and brought him on to see his friends and to give me a chance to see him. He came. I saw. And he conquered. A rare man was Henry Hurd. But I have referred to him elsewhere. And I hope to see him in heaven. What blessed thing it is for a minister to be such a man and such a preacher and such a pastor as to win the hearts of old and young, to fill the whole neighborhood with his memory, and to awaken a desire in the hearts of people to find "a home in heaven with the hope of seeing *him* once more"! Of him I must write more fully.

I do not look back with any enthusiasm on my own work in North Belleville. But the people did a good work for me and made me ambitious to be a more faithful pastor and a great deal better preacher than I ever had been or (to confess the whole truth) far better than I have any expectation of ever becoming.

After two happy years in North Belleville I was sent to Camptown, a small charge near to Newark. While I was there the name was changed to "Irvington." It is but a short distance from Newark; indeed, I expect someone who reads this report will write to me that Irvington is now a part of Newark. Well, so it was, practically, in "my day," and a pleasant place it was to me. It seemed a little nearer to New York than North Belleville. The church there was a neat building, the people had their ambitions, and their ideals, and wanted Methodism to "hold its own socially" and all that. The Reformed Dutch Church had a hold there, and a good many people who belonged to "the best society," whatever that is, went to the Dutch Church. But I found some very lovely people and every way worthy, in both the Churches, and as I was a strenuous member of "the Holy Catholic Church" and believed in a spirit of good will and a holy rivalry, and as I had never known any "society" that I accounted as above me, and supposed that to aspire and to attain and to help others to look up and to reach up and to climb up is a part of the work of the Church, I took for granted that all that the pastor had to do was to rise up and to urge his flock to lay hold of all the really better things within reach; and during my pastorate in Irvington I had the pleasure of numbering among my best friends people of all the Churches – the Baileys and the Bruens and the Browns – but I must *not* call the roll!

I boarded most of the time with the Rathbones and the Driscolls, and by both I was treated as a brother. In Irvington, too, were the Browns. Albert Brown was a preacher – a local preacher – scholarly, a bit, the slightest bit, fanatical on two or three subjects – but as courageous as any soldier and with a fine sense of humor which he vainly tried (through a mistaken idea as to what holiness is) to repress. But his divinely imparted genius for the bright and felicitous and witty thing could never be overcome by his sense of awe or his notions about laughter and mischief and solemnity and the like. Dear fellow he was! How I do want to see him again! I'm almost afraid he will have lost his felicitous lisp, and his ready flash of humor (often at his own expense) and his keen sense of the ludicrous. But I suppose that such things won't count in the felicities and fellowships of heaven. And the lack of them won't be noticed. But I do want to see and greet the genial, the generous, the earnest, the reverent, and the loving Albert Brown again. I am so sure that he is in heaven that I account one of the joys of the Celestial City the fellowship of dear Albert.

It was in Irvington that I began what was one of the most valuable devices or organizations of all my pastoral career – the Palestine Class. Wherever I served as pastor after that (with but one exception) I organized a Palestine Class, and it always proved a help in my entire work as pastor, teacher, and preacher.

The Palestine Class was a Saturday afternoon meeting in my church for the young and old, for members of my own and such persons as cared to come from all the other Churches and congregations in the town or neighborhood. I had such a class in Irvington, N. J., in Joliet, Mount Morris, Galena, and Rockford, Ill. It was devoted to study of sacred history, geography, and biography. In a series of questions and answers the course covered the whole outline of Bible history from "The Creation" to the "Story of St. John" on Patmos.

To help the memory, all the Bible places – countries, mountains, waters, etc. – were arranged in chants for rhythmic, rapid repetition, so that by the aid of an outline map, with no name in sight, the class might easily become familiar with the entire field of sacred geography. The simultaneous repetition, the rhythmic movement, and the strong body of sound fixed the whole field of sacred history, biography and geography in the memory. It made the Saturday afternoon study like a pleasant play and attracted the old as well as the young. To ensure thoroughness every individual was subjected to an examination and was promoted from grade to grade, first a "Pilgrim to Palestine," then having passed the required examination he was made a "Resident" in Palestine, and was assigned to one town for all information, concerning which the class held its "resident" responsible. Continuing the course of study, the "Resident" became "Explorer" of one of the other Biblical regions, and then as the interest of the historic development centered in Jerusalem, the "Explorer" became a "Dweller in Jerusalem," and finally a "Templar." And in my later classes every "Templar" received a gold medal. Beyond that was the grade of "High Templar."

The Palestine Class became a delightful fraternity (more nearly a "sorosis" than a "fraternity"), and how full it was of enthusiasm! In these days I occasionally meet members of the old Palestine Classes. I hope to meet them in the heavenly Jerusalem. Representatives are still living of my classes in Irvington, N. J., Joliet, Mount Morris, Galena, and Rockford, in Illinois. Any one of them reading these lines can greatly cheer their old teacher by a line of recognition. May we all meet in the New Jerusalem!

Distinguished persons when they die are sure to receive attention from the press. Attention is called to the field they occupied and the work they accomplished. But many a saint whose life, character, and example have enriched the humble sphere in which he lived is remembered only by the few who knew him. But how often such retiring and quiet lives exert a far greater influence than do many of the distinguished characters about whom the press publishes brilliant panegyrics.

It is fitting to honor in this way distinguished representatives of state and Church. It does the living good to be reminded of the words and deeds of the worthy dead. But how easily after this imposing way of remembering we may forget.

But a worthy father and a devoted mother one continues to remember and can never forget. These closer and more tender ties hold firmly after all the flowers have faded. The tears come after twenty or thirty or fifty years, as we stand by the spot where only the dust remains. We remember and think, and our hearts burn within us. We need no photograph, no portrait to remind us. We carry within our souls a living picture of those we call the dead.

Two such pictures, belonging to the years 1852 and 1854, deserve a place in the records I am now making. They were strong factors in my life. I love them both to-day as I did nearly sixty years ago. One was a woman – my mother. The other was a friend whom I did not even know when my mother died – a minister of the gospel, young, earnest, spiritual (and *spirituelle,* as well) who lived on the heights. He walked with God. These two personalities did more for me in the fashioning of my ideals and the enriching of my life before I was thirty-three years of age than all the teachers in all the school years of my youth.

The first of these was my mother. It was in 1852 that she left us. She was a rare woman. She was not remarkable in an intellectual or literary way. She was a plain, simple-hearted, upright, sincere Christian to whom Christ was more than a name to be spelled in capital letters and to be honored as the founder of a faith. She needed no arguments out of the books to sustain her creed. She wore no golden cross on her breast as an ornament nor as a symbol of her faith. She entered into no argument to establish any proposition made in her religious profession, nor did those who knew her best need any profession on her part as to the reality of the gospel she believed. When in class meeting, she gave her testimony it was in a quiet, soft-voiced way. She was naturally very timid. But she gave her testimony simply, distinctly, humbly, and all who knew her, from father to housemaid, listened attentively to her words and believed them, and believed the more in the Christ she represented, because they knew how consistently, humbly, steadily in all the outgoings of her personal character and unconscious influence she did stand for the words Christ spoke, whether they were words of promise or command.

My mother was not a highly educated nor in any sense a literary woman, but she was a daily and diligent reader of the Bible. She read and reread the lives of Bramwell, Carvosso, Harlan Page, Lady Huntington [sic], Lady Maxwell, John and Mary Fletcher, Hervey's "Meditations," Baxter's "Saints' Rest," the little monographs (then being for the first time published) on the "Second Blessing," and kindred topics by Mrs. Phebe [sic] Palmer of New York.

She visited the sick in her neighborhood and treated her servants as though she and they were sisters of charity. She dressed plainly, really with Quaker simplicity, and perfectly illustrated the emphases of the most intelligent and earnest of the old-time Methodists: plainness, neatness, economy, silence, charity, prayerfulness. She conscientiously gave her testimony in general class and love feast to the reality of the life of faith, and all who knew her loved to hear her speak.

My mother's father was a sea captain, Bernard Raser. He died in the West Indies. One of our most prized family treasures is his portrait on ivory, painted in Paris. In his fine face one sees the repose and amiability which his daughter so beautifully illustrated in her devoted and beautiful life.

As a home keeper she was neatness, frugality, carefulness, hospitality incarnate, and the perfection of self-sacrifice where the well-being of others was in any way concerned. She was a woman of good sense and a living illustration of the power and beauty of the divine grace. Her daily walk was without weakness or wavering. On the human side she had everything to command respect, confidence, and affection. And into this human life came the steady, pure, and transfiguring currents of the divine love. And she did have communion with God.

There was one habit which mother adopted when her children were very young which she kept up until within a few weeks of her death. On every Sabbath evening, after the usual season of singing and prayer at the regular family devotions, she would lead us, her four children, into her own room and there spend a few minutes in a plain, practical talk, and then she would offer a brief prayer. In the twilight, the moonlight, or the dense darkness we always found our way to the place of the Sunday evening prayer. How penetrating and heart-searching were her questions and appeals! It was indeed the holy of holies.

I purposed to tell the story of her death, but in our times less stress is placed by the average Christian on the last hours and the experience of the dying saint. It is possible that the conditions of the last hours are not favorable to the most satisfactory testimony which the dying saint may give or is expected to give. But to my mind the hour of departure may be opportunity for farewell words not only full of peace but burdened with messages of warning and counsel and comfort to those who are left behind. One thing I may say, that my mother was a firm believer in the reality of the eternal life and the power of the divine grace to sustain, comfort, and give victory even in the valley and shadow of death. Mother died as she lived, witnessing to the reality of her faith in Christ, his gospel, victory over fear, and perfect confidence in the open gate, the crown of life, the vision of Christ, and the continuing city.

The second of the influential factors in my early ministerial life about whom in this chapter I desire to write was one of my predecessors in the pastorate of North Belleville in the old New Jersey Conference. It is now Nutley.

Henry Hurd had been pastor of North Belleville, and when I first reached the place as pastor his praises were on everybody's tongue. He was talked about so much by old and young and praised so enthusiastically that I resolved to become acquainted with him. His health had been seriously impaired, and he had spent some time at Dr. Jackson's water cure in central New York. I persuaded him to pay his old parishioners at North Belleville a little visit. He came and was warmly welcomed by the people and by their pastor. He captured me at once. His liberality, breadth, earnestness, and openness of mind attracted me, and we became intimate friends. He had spent some time at Dr. Jackson's water cure in central New York and had caught a glimpse of views and interpretations not usually held in those days. He had come to think that the realm of spirit may be under the sway of forces and subject to laws as really as the realm of matter, and that as there is a science of the material so there is possible a science of spirit. It was a mild form of Swedenborgianism, and was as loyal to Christ and as positive in its recognition of the reign of law in the spiritual as any scientist's view of the fact of law in the realm of matter. It was practically what Henry Drummond sets forth in his monograph on "Natural Law in the Spiritual World."

What most thoughtful believers now accept as true was by many in those early years branded as heresy. Henry Hurd recognized the realm of spirit as under law and subject to forces of divine energy which could be depended upon as really as the forces of the material world. He believed in the science of a spiritual life.

Of all the friends of my early ministerial life Henry Hurd was the most stimulating, especially in the line of the subjective spiritual experience. There is a science of the spiritual life. And I believe that so-called "Christian Science" has its hold upon many people because of the stress it lays on the scientific element in religion, an emphasis made with such skill and ingenuity by Henry Drummond. And Robertson does the same thing. Henry Hurd used to recognize the place of the scientific method in the interpretation of the spiritual world, and of the personal spiritual experience.

The memory of Henry Hurd is an inspiration to me to this day. He was a most attractive fellow, refined and strong. His face and blue eyes were full of light. He had a voice of rare sweetness, depth, clearness, force, and was what we call magnetic. He was an idealist in the highest and best sense. He was in sympathy with all teachers of Christian truth who exalted Christ and who sought to interpret in a scientific way and spirit the processes by which Christ seeks to possess and dominate the spiritual life of the humble believer.

In my private journal for March 20, 1854, I find this record: "The fellowship with Hurd continues. He says, 'God is truth. Live by the truth. Cultivate temperance. Take exercise. Think of God. Pray. Resist temptation. Converse on religious subjects. Avoid wandering thoughts.'"

Some of his utterances at the last were reported to me by his wife. While at Glen Haven water cure (I think it was) and where he died, he said, "It would be sweet to go out by the lake and breathe the fresh air. It is more pleasant to lie here and suffer God's will. If it is God's will I shall live, I will bless him." When later the doctor told him that he could not live, he said, "Now it is settled that I go,

I shall look forward to my dissolution with joyful anticipation." He spoke of death with a sweet smile and said, "It is going home." Again he said, "I die in full view of heaven and with the assurance of entering there . ***

[2] I regret that I cannot enter on higher ground." Referring to an experience of the day before, he said, "I understand what it is to be filled with all the fullness of God and I am almost impatient to be gone. But that is not right. I must not be impatient." Then he said, "Only think of being ushered into the glories of heaven in one short hour."

He left to me the works of Dr. Chalmers,[3] because, said he, "I prize them more than any other of my theological works." A few minutes before his death he said, in reply to his wife's request for a last message, "Carey, lead a true life, a true life."

At the last he said, "I retain all my senses." When he could no longer speak, he nodded his head to several questions. He died between eleven and twelve o'clock on Friday morning, October 6, 1854. In my journal for that day I made the record, "He was the best man I ever knew and the best friend I ever had."

2. This mark is in the original publication.
3. Scottish moral philosopher and Natural Theologian Thomas Chalmers, 1780-1847.

CHAPTER 16

# The Autobiography of Bishop Vincent

# Thirteenth Paper[1]

***July 6, 1910***

At a very early age I took to preaching. My mother used to tell about my first essays in this line as in Alabama I would gather the little negroes and the white children of the neighborhood and preach to them. I loved to play the preacher. And I always conducted the singing. No, there was no "taste" for religion in it. It was a passion for "speaking in public," and being "like the preacher." It was nothing but "play," the form of self-gratification that appealed to me. I had a good voice and an early ambition "to be a preacher." I was brought up with the understanding that the ministry was my "calling." And it pleased my sweet and godly mother to think that I was called to that field of service. But it did not mean that I was a peculiarly "good boy" with a "heavenly calling" already recognized and accepted. For I was not a good boy. I was ambitious, had strong self-will, loved praise, was not always absolutely truthful, was easily alarmed by the thought of death, used to dream about the judgment day, and "the great white throne," and in my dreams I was usually on the "left side" of the Judge. More than once as a little fellow I woke

1. *Northwestern Christian Advocate,* Vol. 58, No. 27, pages 10-11.

from a dreadful dream and found myself in perspiration, with all the terrors of despair in my little trembling soul. Our preachers dealt with the dark side of destiny in those days. No, it cannot be said that they neglected the ethical side of everyday life nor that they failed to present the cheerful and gladsome side of life present and eternal, but "the law" with its ideals, it positive claims, required the preaching also of the penalties attached to its violation. And it was by *alarming* people that they were persuaded to look for "salvation," which was usually understood to be *safety* and *happiness* present and eternal, and all this through the mediation of Jesus who had died for mankind and who is now ready, willing, and even eager to give to all life, peace, pardon, the joy of present and the hope of future and eternal salvation.

I should be untrue to the facts not to acknowledge that too often the preacher's emphasis *was* on "personal safety" and "personal happiness" and the certainty of "a home in heaven." And I dare not deny that it is easily possible to put such emphasis on personal safety as to transform the whole of a religious effort into a process of "selfish" endeavor. After such exciting of alarm it is easy to appeal to self-interest as to allay all alarm for the nonce, and give the "seeker" of religion a sense of security and a feeling of "peace" and then to sing the "doxology" over him as though the miracle of supernatural transformation had actually been wrought in his case. Then comes the "counting" and the report to the papers, and soon there come doubt, reaction, tacit regret, silence – and the old life is resumed. Then after "wonder" comes, very often, a type of post-revival apathy that is almost like death. But the "arithmetic" remains.

But dare I leave the situation, dismal as it is, without another word? Do I mean by this picture of revivalism to condemn special efforts for the persuasion of sinners to accept Christ? Certainly, I do not. But I do mean to urge upon all ministers of the gospel and all "evangelists" and especially upon all intelligent parents and pastors to safeguard our young people and all "outsiders" against everything that savors of superficiality and sensationalism in the attempt to commit them to the "profession of religion." Teach plainly and wisely and with earnest emphasis the great doctrines of theology. Don't aim primarily at producing a state, a mood of alarm. Put the truth concerning God and law and biblical ideals of everyday life. Preach Christ as God's ideal of manhood, Christ as God's expression of the sweetest, tenderest, holiest possibilities of human life, Christ as the solution of every problem that can be raised concerning the possibility of pardon, the power of the divine energies applied to the weak and wicked soul of man, Christ as the key to the unlocking of all the problems of the social order and the social future. Don't aim to scare, to terrorize people, especially little people and nervous and over sensitive people. It is easily possible to so alarm a human personality as to disturb his moral equilibrium and make his "decisions" absolutely worthless as [he] steps toward a genuine and vigorous life. The whole process may be damaging to the ethical as well as to the more delicate spiritual sense of the individual whose "soul" we are trying to save. The terrors of the law may have their place, but they do not "convert" people. Terror may arrest attention. So far so good. But terror must be allayed before its subject is able calmly, deliberately, and effectively to make the choice that tells on *character*. A sense of sin and a loathing of it – that is one thing. But personal anxiety about one's personal "safety" may most seriously interfere with character-making resolve.

Therefore, we should approach our candidates for the blessed work of "salvation" with great care, wisdom, calmness, and with an honest effort to prevent excessive excitement. It is very easy just here to turn upon the sane counselor who seeks to secure calmness and seriousness in order to make sure that the seeker after God under his care deliberately, positively, intelligently *chooses for eternity*, chooses rationally, chooses with his eyes wide open – it is very easy to say to such wise adviser, "Hands off – let that soul alone." But if ever or at any time wise counsel by an experienced teacher is needed, it is just here and now as a soul looks and listens for the Heavenly Father's guidance. Superficiality at this crisis in the history of a soul is a crime. Hence the importance of quiet, calmness, thoughtfulness, wisdom "in the inquiry room" or "at the altar."

What has this to do with the writer's autobiography? Much every way. In my experience as a pastor I was sorely perplexed because I could not, as so many of my brethren did, "conduct a revival" and report large numbers as the result of "evangelistic endeavor," nor have I been able to unite with many most earnest and excellent "evangelists" who have seemed to put such stress on "feeling badly" and then "feeling better" and then "arithmetic" and then apathy and "arrested development."

I trust that this plain statement of the case, inevitable if I am to tell the whole truth in the attempt at telling the story of my life, will not be interpreted as an expression of "opposition to revivals." *I am not opposed to revivals.* But I am opposed to all superficiality, and spasmodic effort as a substitute for calm, rational, intelligent, unremitting endeavor for twelve months every year, to enlighten every community concerning the realities of religion, to appeal to the impenitent, to show an interest, a constant interest, during the whole year, in the spiritual well-being of everybody for whose enlightenment we are responsible. I plead for the pastoral carefulness and watchfulness that will lead the unconverted who pass our church any day of the year to think of it as a Church that is all the while seeking to bring sinners to God, and to build up believers in God.

So often in my advocacy of this law of continuity and steadiness I have been grossly misrepresented that I use this, my last opportunity to declare my faith in 365 days a year of earnest work in behalf of the building up of believers in their holy faith, that they may labor in one way or another for 365 days every year to help each other in such upbuilding, and to persuade the neglectful ones of the community in which they live, to unite with them in the service of God and in the bringing in of his kingdom. And I plead for that wisdom and fidelity that will use *special seasons* and *special opportunities* for winning the outsiders to the service of Christ. It is only when the Church is faithful to its trust all the year that it has a right to hope for the largest success from such special endeavors.

One of the most important features of Church work is the use of the laity in the work of instruction and the exalting of education as a part of the mission of the Church. The Sunday School has contributed very largely to the increase of Bible study by the people. But a great deal remains to be done. The best work of the Sunday School is not done in the class by the teacher but by the individual pupil at home as he or she prepares for the recitation of next Sunday, but when at home every pupil teaches the lesson of next Sunday to somebody else, a younger brother or sister, the girl in the kitchen, the neighbor old or young who needs such assistance, then the lesson is really doing some good and the pupil who helps somebody else is "preparing the lesson" in the very best possible way.

It is by such cooperative and continuous work of Bible study that the Church is to be built up, numbers increased, workers multiplied, and the whole Church led to work all the time for the promotion of Bible study throughout the entire community.

And one other thing is greatly needed, more than any other thing in pulpit, home, and Sunday School class, and that is a *real* faith, a faith that grapples brain and heart and will, and all the executive faculties of personality while the preaching and the teaching processes are going on. This is the "one thing" above every other thing in the while series of agencies and processes connected with home, pulpit, and Sunday School life. Good God: Awaken us thy servants to this one pressing, imperative, and supreme need of thy Church!

For many years while in the pastorate and in my special efforts to create a general interest in the training of Sunday School teachers and officers, I held in all parts of the country institutes and normal classes after the general plan of the secular educators. In this work I had the sympathy and cooperation of Mr. Lewis Miller of Akron, O., an energetic and aggressive Sunday School worker, the head of the famous and admirable Akron Sunday School, and it was at his suggestion that I consented to take one of my Sunday School Institutes to Chautauqua. I gave it the name of "assembly" to distinguish it from the ordinary Sunday School conventions and institutes. It was a new use of the term "assembly" and enabled its managers to present to the public a new experiment. The camp meeting management at Fairpoint on the shores of Lake Chautauqua, through the influence of the president of the camp meeting association, Mr. Lewis Miller of Akron, O., allowed us to use their grounds for two weeks in August, 1874. He as president took charge of the business side and I as superintendent of instruction took into my hands the details of the platform and the educational side of the movement. It proved to be a great success. Year after year the assembly has held its sessions, opening as the assembly on the first Tuesday evening of August and gradually extending its programs and aims until it covers practically the months of July and August. The story of the inception, development, and present scope of the Chautauqua Assembly is told in *The Chautauqua Movement*, by the writer of these lines, and also in a most interesting little volume by Editor Bray of *The Chautauquan*.

Perhaps the most radical and permanent of the various devices which Chautauqua has presented to the public is familiarly known as "The C. L. S. C.," that is, "The Chautauqua Literary and Scientific Circle," a device for promoting reading at home, especially by adults – the "out-of-school folks" – who having outgrown the regular day-school age may pursue at home, as adults' courses of reading and study "just as though they were still girls and boys" and may be "at school" as in the other years. This "C. L. S. C. course of reading" is designed to be a school at home for the grown-up and old folks, many of whom are just as eager to be students to-day as they forty, fifty, or more years ago. And these older readers make the best kind of "students" because they know now the value of education and they know practical life, which is of immense service to one who takes up a book for the sake of getting good out of it. A man or woman of fifty or sixty years of age, in ordinary health, will make a wiser use of a book than any young person can. For years it was thought by many people that educational opportunities are limited to the early years of life. But we find that maturity is more likely to *think* for itself about what it reads than is youth. And to start an adult from thirty to eighty years of age on a course of reading and study is to do vastly more good to homes and society at large than people used to think. The Chautauqua Literary and Scientific Circle has enrolled tens of thousands of names of middle-aged and old people, men and women, parents and grandparents who have taken up and carried through for from four to fourteen and more years, courses of reading in science, political economy, literature, art, and philosophy, and the fact of enrollment in an "institution," the fact of association with "other students," a curriculum provided, and an "end" of the "course" in view – all these elements appeal to ambitious people who still foster "ideals" who in good health although no longer young, hope and resolve to go on and on and up and "higher yet" until they shall be accounted among those "who are worthy to be crowned." Tens of thousands of adult readers from thirty to ninety years of age have pursued the "college-outlook" course of the C. L. S. C., and the joy and sense of "pride" of the right kind thus developed one may read on the faces of that "chosen company" which at Chautauqua, on Recognition Day, marches through the "Golden Gate" and between the rows of flower scattering maidens, under arch after arch with their hearts athrob and their faces radiant. It is a great thing to put hope into an old heart.[2] It is a noble thing to guide earnest and eager old folks into ways of living and thinking that will lengthen, enliven, brighten, and beautify the period of life we call in our mistaken conception of it "dotage." Chautauqua contributes to the sweet picture of old age as described by Madame de Stael,[3] "When a noble life has prepared old age, it is not the decline that it reveals, but the first days of immortality."

The dream of Chautauqua which would make parents and other grown-up folks who have not had much to do with "the higher education" familiar with the world of culture – the university world – is not as impracticable as the superficial view of it

2. Recognition Day at Chautauqua Institution is the annual commencement day for graduates of the C. L. S. C. The march described is the traditional procession through the grounds prior to the awarding of diplomas.
3. French writer Madame de Stael (Germain Neckar), (1766-1817).

may lead one to think. Thousands of homes never think of training their boys and girls to consider the college as the gateway into the "wide, wide world." Trades, business, a chance to make a living and to accumulate a fortune – that is the main thing. Of course if a fellow is be a lawyer or a preacher or a teacher or a doctor it would be well for him "to go to college," but what does a business man, a fellow in for a big fortune, what is the use of college for him? Now that is the way the average money-seeking machine of a man reasons: scholarship for the learned professions, but for business learn the art of money-making and let "learning" go "to the dogs" and to the "dons." If the main idea of life be to accumulate fortunes, to "enjoy life" to go "into society," why waste time and money on "culture"? The real enjoyment of modern society of a certain type does not require what you call "culture." You may dance and play cards and spend five nights a week at the theater, you may dine and wine and smoke at will and nobody cares what you know about science, or about pictures, or about archeology or philosophy or sociology.

All this I have been talking about represents a type of society life – a very frivolous and empty type. But Chautauqua and the Church and the true university care very little for such life.

The life that is worthwhile is a life that keeps in mind the whole of life: Physical, intellectual, industrial, ethical, spiritual, social, political, philanthropical, the life present and temporal and the life eternal.

The Chautauqua idea embraces the ideal life of culture as all-comprehensive and again as the privilege of all classes of people. Those two thoughts are the Chautauqua thoughts. Seek the largest attainable culture – whoever you are, in order to do this. Read widely to discover your measure of capacity and power. Find out what your tastes and capacities and abilities are and give yourself to the noble task of self-culture, in harmony with your ability and opportunity.

In this Chautauqua is in the true sense of the word democratic. It urges upon all people, everywhere, to seek self-knowledge and then self-culture. If you are poor, dependent upon your own exertions for all that you get – food, clothing, occupation, opportunity – resolve to be, to know, to grow, to get, to achieve. Be a student. Be a doer of worthy deeds. Be a thinker. Learn how to express yourself, by tongue and by pen. Work, economize, think your way out of difficulty. Overcome opposition. All such effort being the exercise of will develops will power. And this is "education" at its best.

It is a very beautiful device educational – this Chautauqua plan by which a man or woman, young or old, in town or country, may turn the whole of life, with its manual labor, its brief moments of leisure, its time at the table, "twenty minutes" earlier rising in the morning, its act of private prayer, the reading of the morning paper, the casual conversation conducted deliberately, the habit of thinking and thinking and *thinking* – all turned into self-discipline, until one gets into the habit of using his powers intellectual under the control of the will, and thus every day grows in knowledge, in self-mastery, in power of concentration, in the habit of looking at things until seeing through them one becomes an example to his neighbors and an inspiration to them, and especially to the young life of the community.

The habit thus gradually formed grows into a passion, and dullness makes way for ambition and the plodding "laboring man" becomes an enthusiast in the pursuit of knowledge. Of course it is practicable. It requires the talent of "a resolve," and then easily and surely come "two" talents and then "five" and at last "ten." All this is what Chautauqua stands for.

The Chautauqua movement is the most effective way of building up the college and the university. It educates parents. Thus, it incites parents to be interested in the public school and the press. It ensures better books in the home and in the neighborhood library. It puts the college directly across the path of life and trains youth to seek a broader culture before entering into practical, permanent life pursuits. The C. L. S. C. is usually presented as a condensation of the college student's wide outlook on the world of history, literature, science, art, human nature, and political economy, so that adults, parents at home, mechanics, business men, energetic and earnest women – especially mothers, may cover the fields of college work and thus keep as loving companions in steady fellowship with their more favored sons and daughters, living within the same broad and rich horizon, finding a common interest and a growing delight in the fields of modern culture.

CHAPTER 17

# The Autobiography of Bishop Vincent

## Fourteenth Paper[1]

*July 13, 1910*

My father having settled in Chicago in the late "fifties" and having been placed there in charge of the Western branch of the firm of Vincent, Himrod & Co. – the Vincent at the head of firm being Mr. B. B. Vincent of Erie, Pa., (a cousin of my father) – it was natural that I should respond to my father's invitation to "come West." After weighing the matter carefully I submitted the question to the proper ecclesiastical authorities, and was transferred to the Rock River Conference and stationed at Joliet, which "charge" had about that time been vacated by the transfer of its incumbent – Rev. William Goodfellow – to South America. It was in May, 1857, that this transfer to the West was effected and that I was appointed to Joliet. My home was in the family of Mr. Otis Hardy, one of the wisest and best Methodist laymen I ever knew.

I was a comparatively young man, but recently from the East, and was in Illinois to take charge of a pulpit which had been occupied by some of the strongest men of the Rock River Conference. Among the laymen of the Church, in addition to Otis Hardy were

1. *Northwestern Christian Advocate*, Vol. 58, No. 28, pages 10-11.

Mr. Cassiday, Mr. Niece, Mr. Mack, and Hugh Norwood. I was a young man, something of a student, ambitious and eager to make a "success." I engaged in the work with the highest and best motives I could command. I trust that while the human incentives were present there was also an earnest desire to do good work for the glory of God and the benefit of those committed to my care.

One of the most interesting men of Joliet at that time was Dr. Danforth, a practicing physician, who had strong sympathy with our Church although not in any sense a Methodist. He was rather inclined to the "New Church" or Swedenborgian ideas. He was a great reader, a fine talker, and on the whole an entertaining man. It was through him that I became acquainted with the views of Emanuel Swedenborg. I read the Swedish seer to some extent and was impressed, as I think most readers of his works are, with the strong emphasis he places on the harmony between the world of matter and the world of spirit. I found much to interest me in his doctrine of "correspondence" – a doctrine which emphasizes the reality of forces and phenomena in the realm of the spirit under law, as are the forces and phenomena in the world of matter. There is a great truth hidden away in the "Science of Correspondence." What errors may be lodged in the system it is not my purpose now to inquire. But it was in Joliet and in my acquaintance with Dr. Danforth that I first learned the outlines of the theories of the Swedish seer. I never went any further in my investigations than to grasp the conception of the Swedenborgian as to the correspondence between the world of matter and the world of spirit, and both as the expression and illustration of the divine wisdom and love and power. Going that far I have found it helpful in the interpretation of the Word of God in the book of nature and in the Book of Revelation.

### *The Model Layman*

I have spoken of Otis Hardy. He was a wise man – one of the best of men. His education was limited. He was very "conservative." He was very strongly attached to the old Methodist processes. But he was a rare man in many ways. He was unselfish, sympathetic, philanthropic, positive in his convictions, but ready to "hear the other side." He was loyal to his pastor, anxious to see his church prosper, open to conviction, and it was most interesting to watch the effect of new and "progressive" ideas on him. He was hesitant when a new thought was suggested. He was cautious, quiet, thoughtful, prayerful, practical, naturally inclined to be what we call "narrow;" but the first thing his friends knew he had adopted some new or advanced theory of Church life and work and was anxious to "give it a chance" so as to see "how it would go." Otis Hardy was one of the most benevolent, fairest, kindest, and most consecrated men I ever knew. In the life beyond, where the language of Zion is spoken, and where life is the perpetual and perfect interpretation of ruling motive and reigning love, Otis Hardy will be like a master and a leader, as he was here in life and conduct, and an illustration of the best there is in the gospel of our Lord and Saviour Jesus Christ.

I could say many cordial things about Mr. Cassiday and our delightful Sunday School superintendent, Hugh Norwood. They wrought well in their day and have gone to their blessed reward. The hospitality of the one and the skill of the other are recorded in the book of remembrance.

It was in Joliet that I made my first Western experiment with my Palestine Class idea. It proved a great success in Joliet as it had in New Jersey and as it afterward [did] in Mount Morris, Galena, and Rockford. Every Saturday afternoon the lecture room was filled for two hours or more with old and young, representing all the denominations, engaged in the study of sacred history and biography and with special emphasis on geography, using the old method of chanting to aid the memory; and then every pupil was subjected to a thorough examination to make sure that what was memorized through chant and song and simultaneous recitation was thoroughly understood by the individual pupil. The Palestine class in Joliet, as elsewhere, tended to promote unity among the various denominations. I also organized in Joliet a successful normal class for the training of Sunday School teachers.

My appointment to Mount Morris after my initiation in Joliet into the western field was greatly to my liking. It was the seat of a seminary, which fact gave me hope and really a promise of educational opportunity which I greatly coveted. There I might find stimulus in personal study, contact with the professors, incentive to most earnest endeavor in the presence of a large number of students, life in the country practically both a "circuit" and a "station," with opportunity for pastoral work among farmers as well as among the people of the town. All that I dreamed of and hoped for were realized in my single year at Mount Morris. I boarded with the excellent Fred Brayton, his intelligent wife, his positive, aggressive, and faithful mother, his interesting, affectionate children. And to that home I took my bride, my now sorely lamented "Elizabeth."[2]

2. Sarah Elizabeth Dusenbury Vincent died in 1909 as Bishop Vincent was compiling his reminiscences.

## *A College Community*

The Mount Morris appointment was for me opportunity for the prosecution of certain lines of study, for contact with men and women who in a way represented "the higher education." It gave a chance to study eager, irrepressible, and impressible young life, and it was a happy blending of town and country. There were the aggressiveness and ambitions of the one and the simplicity, teachableness, and warm-heartedness of the other. I used the opportunity for taking private lessons in New Testament Greek, listened to all the lectures that were offered, conversed (with a student's undeclared purpose) with the most intelligent and scholarly persons I could find, made all my sermons opportunity for a sort of "recitation," eliciting modestly and honestly and often successfully the frank "criticism" of the "best thinkers" in my congregation, studying critically for myself the persons who were called "scholars," and those turned my public and official work into the best kind of educational opportunity. It did me a world of good. The students by their presence and attention stimulated me to do my best; the sharp questions and hints and occasional semi-sarcastic observations of one of the old "retired" professors (for whom I had not only respect but a genuine "fear") put me on my guard and made me revise many a passage I thought of putting "into my sermon next Sunday." It was a veritable "school" for me, that year in the Mount Morris pulpit, with Principal Harlow and Professors Hale and Pope and ex-Professor Pinckney and two or three bright women – teachers themselves and readers in wide ranges of literature – all these in my congregations and a lot of students beside who were preparing to be professional critics, and who (some of them) did become specialists in science, in literature, in politics, and in business.

The denominational seminary has not outgrown its mission. It is of great value to the local community and to the patronizing and sustaining denomination. It advertises the college and the university. It is a postgraduate school for the high school graduate and at the same time a preparatory school for the college. It ensures a greater degree of thoroughness in the freshman, preparing him for the peculiar student conditions which have so much to with the first year of college life and is in a certain sense a protection against the perils of the freshman. Its graduate is already initiated into the distinctive life of the college student. He is prepared to begin wisely and safely the collegian's career, to save time and to enter full-fledged the life for which the college stands.

The location of the old Rock River Seminary was a very fine one – in the heart of an exceptionally rich farming section, easy of access from every part of northern Illinois and southern Wisconsin, elevated, occupying a "mountain height," healthful, and literally "beautiful for situation." I should not like to be the man who suggested, and much less the man who urged the abandonment of Mount Morris as a Methodist center of education. But I am sure that by this time that man must be dead!

One of the principal characters in Mount Morris at the time of which I write was Professor Pinckney. Years before he was identified with the seminary. Why he left it I never knew. He was a genius with some of the eccentricities that often go with genius. He was brilliant, self-assertive, somewhat sarcastic and severe, really eloquent, perhaps too fond of criticizing the current *regime*, but a man of power, possibly disappointed at not having been more "successful" in getting control of affairs. A wiser and stronger administration might have made a better use of his power.

Principal Harlow was an earnest man, amiable, practical, beloved by his students and a thoroughly consecrated follower of the Christ. He came during the later years of his life into a deeper, richer personal experience. He was always conscientious and faithful, but coming into association with advocates of the *boundary line* conception of "holiness," he embraced it and, so far as I have ever known, he really illustrated it by calmness of spirit, sanity of definition, and consistency of conduct.

Thinking about the old seminary at Mount Morris starts the question in my mind as to how far these midway schools (the higher academics, the seminaries, the high schools of our public school system) are contributing to the college and university as they ought and so easily might do. There are scores and hundreds of graduates from the high school who might so easily be persuaded to continue their educational career after graduation by entering some college and gaining more thorough training. There are so many and great advantages in what we call a "liberal education" that more should be made of it by parents, teachers, and foremost and influential citizens. There is no need of this haste to be "in business," this eagerness to enter prematurely into "man's estate." It is better to be "better prepared" for the work which men and women are so eager to undertake. A mechanic has great advantages in every way if as a mechanic he is also a *man*, a thinking, reading, broadened, self-knowing, and self-governed man who is not only qualified for a trade, an "occupation, "a specialty," but who is a citizen with the sense of personal, political, and social responsibility pressing upon him. To be an intelligent, independent voter in the United States is quite as important as to be able to "make a living" and to "get along" and to "rise," as we are in the habit of putting it.

We need to-day an evangelism of culture to hold our young life for a longer time in the public school and to make easy for every boy and girl the pathway from the high school to the college.

Home should be awakened to the importance of this, and the public school teachers and all of our preachers and pastors should be stirred up to a mission in behalf of "the higher education." A servant girl who has literary taste, a love for books, an appreciation of pictures, and who while she works in the kitchen revels in the realm of high and noble thought and now and then breaks out into song or prayer simply transforms her sphere into a paradise, and while she serves with skill and exquisite taste she walks "on the high places" of time, and is in training for the felicities and royal fellowships of the eternal heavens. It was while Jesus "washed the feet" of his disciples that the inspired evangelist records the fact of his high preparation for that lowly ministry: "And Jesus knowing that he came from God and that he went to God, supper being ended, he washed the feet of his disciples."[3]

Let us live for the culture of the whole of society from plough-boy to president, from cook to queen.

3. See John 13:1-17.

CHAPTER 18

# The Autobiography of Bishop Vincent

## Fifteenth Paper[1]

***July 20, 1910***

It was a great surprise to me when at the annual conference of 1859, on October 10, my name was read out by the bishop for Galena. I had been preacher in charge of Mount Morris for only one year, and I had greatly enjoyed its quiet, its rare opportunity for study, its delightful social advantages with the faculty of the old Rock River Seminary, the families which had been attracted to the place because of its educational facilities, and the young, eager, and earnest students who made it for the time a home. I seemed adapted to the place because of this young life especially, and it was to me like being "at college," for I had laid out a course of study in pursuance of an old plan to "cover the college student's outlook" and to gain mental power by turning all my pulpit and pastoral work into opportunity for mental concentration and self-control. It was, from the conference point of view, a promotion for me, and of course I was glad to have such a field as Galena promised and turned out to be. On Saturday, October 15, I held the last session of my greatly loved Mount Morris Palestine Class. On Sunday I preached from Mark 16:15-18,

1. *Northwestern Christian Advocate,* Vol. 58, No. 29, pages 10-11.

and in the evening from Jer. 8:20. On the Tuesday after I went to Galena and was present at the prayer meeting on Wednesday evening, giving an address on "Prayer" to my new people.

I mention these facts to emphasize the wonderfully practical system of the itinerancy. No Church among us [was] without a pastor for one minute. The incumbent of the present is removed only as the name of his successor is announced. The exceptional cases (death, transfer, change of annual conference relation) are so few that we may safely say that ours is a Church of "the perpetual pastorate."

Galena is one of the oldest and most interesting cities of the old Illinois. The treasures of lead in the region secured an early settlement and the incoming of families of strength and character. The city was once the rival of Chicago. Physically it is the perfect contrast to Chicago. Its high and rugged bluffs, deep ravines, higher levels on both sides of the river that passes through the city on its way to the Mississippi and the Gulf of Mexico, give a variety and charm to the place and make it topographically interesting and beautiful. There is something in the very scenery and in the ruggedness of the place to make Galenians "a peculiar people," zealous in their devotion to the town and its history. Many of the families of Galena are "old families" and were established and "recognized" almost before Chicago was "counted in" as a "city." It had for years had all the ambition of a big city and a municipal pride worthy of a metropolis of larger proportions and greater age. In fact, when Chicago was an infant, Galena was full grown. It had wealth, social life, ambition, representative men could most worthily represent it, and from its situation between the Mississippi and the Lakes, and between the far North and the farther South, it appreciated the great movements of civilization, and its citizens were men of both breadth and enterprise.

Perhaps when I went to Galena to reside there, as the pastor of the old Bench-street Methodist Episcopal Church, the best and palmiest days of Galena were over. But I accounted myself honored by the appointment, and I entered the new field of service with zeal and strong resolve. I was comparatively a young man and was full of ambition. Warmly received by a most cordial people, I gave myself up to the service of the Church and of the community.

There were some choice people in the Bench-street Church: Weigley, an exceptionally gifted man, a lawyer, a genial friend, once a Methodist preacher, a strong personality, an incarnation of good will, and with a touch of sarcasm now and then on his tongue, that but for the smile and glitter of the eyes that accompanied it might easily have hurt and even stung the object of it. And what a lovely family he had, and how loyal they all were to the Church!

What a treat it was now and then to go out to his lovely home for an afternoon; and what a rare pleasure it was to hear him recount his earlier experiences and "take off" some of the specimens of the *genus homo* he had met in the courtroom and elsewhere. He was a good critic and underneath that humor with which he pointed out this or that weak point in somebody's character or the preacher's logic there throbbed a genuine and tender sympathy that made the critic appear, as he really was, the genuine friend of folks in general and of the Church and its mission in particular. How glad I should be to have one more clasp of the hand of the dear Weigley.

Then there was Huntington, steward, Sunday School superintendent, a trustee, and everybody's friend. He was brimful of humor. His was what Richter speaks of as "the laughing cheerfulness that throws the light of day on all the paths of life." And the great-souled and big-bodied Hughlett, who attended Church on Sunday mornings and gave liberally to its support, and entertained preachers and everybody in his great house and indulged his fine daughters and good-hearted son like the prince of a father that he was. No, he did not "go to class meeting." I think I never saw him in prayer meeting. And he is one of the puzzles to the theologians. I am glad that I am not the Judge who determines destiny. If I were – but just here it is time for me to change the subject.

And there is Brother Waggoner of the book store, hospitable as he was strict, taking life a deal more seriously than either Hughlett or Huntington, welcoming Methodist preachers to his home, helping in many ways to build up the Church, and as good-hearted as he was precise and attentive to the minutiae of life. And the Fiddicks – who that has lived in Galena can ever forget them? As American in all that is good as they were English in origin and spirit and representative of a type of English folk who enrich American life by their presence among us. Then there are the Packards – genuine, generous, hospitable, with a rare sense of humor in both wife and husband. The Packards' home was full of cheer. How much time I spent at their glowing fireside. And the Bakers and the Chandlers and then the members of my noble Palestine Class – fifty-eight names are under my eyes as I write this record – fifty-eight "Explorers and their Countries," "from No. 1 Kate Saunders," to "No. 58 Mary Helm." And who can forget the Swifts, with their hospitality, cordiality, Church loyalty, the good father reminding one of St. John, and the girls and their mother and dear George, worthy children of worthy parents? But I have made a mistake in naming any of the dearly beloved Galenians, because I am compelled to omit so many that my heart clamors to make my pen record. As I think the list grows and some picture flashes like a vision within: The Venables, Barrets. Marbles,

Birds, Sacketts, Reeds, Virtues, Ritters, John Nagel, Morgan Lewis – but what is the use of trying to reproduce the whole old Church record? Their names are written in heaven. How I do wish I could name them all here and see them again, and again hear them chant the long lists of Bible names and then after a little prayer shake hands as in the dear old days of 1859-61.

One day, after the farewell given to the soldiers who went to the front during the war of 1861-65, I called on Mrs. Grant. Her husband had raised a company of men and I had just delivered at the railway station a few words of farewell. Calling on Mrs. Grant we got into a bit of a discussion on "North and South, slavery," etc. At last, I said, "Well, Mrs. Grant, we won't discuss this question. I hope your husband will be restored to you in safety." She promptly and with some warmth replied: "Dear me! I hope he'll get to be a major general or something big." I was amused at her courage and ambition and optimism, and not dreaming of any such outcome myself I smiled at her enthusiasm, and at her high opinion of her husband. When in Washington after the close of the war she one day drove me over to see General Rawlings [sic], who was then dying, I reminded her of her confidence in her husband before his war record had justified her high hopes. She promptly replied, "I always knew what was in him if only he had a chance along with the other fellows." Mrs. Grant was a strong woman, refined, accustomed to the best society, outspoken, an ideal mother, a loyal wife, in every way a worthy, positive, interesting woman – a bit abrupt now and then, but always a lady. She was as faithful to her children as she was appreciative of her husband. On the occasion to which I refer, at the general's request in their own home in Washington I baptized their boy Jesse.

General Grant was one of the loveliest and most reverent of men. He had a strong will under that army overcoat of his, but he was the soul of honor and as reverent as he was brave. And he added immortality to the renown the good little city of Galena had already achieved.

It is a great system – this itinerant system of ours. It means a permanent pastorate. It is the perfection of ecclesiastical economy with provision for change when wise counselors agree that change is best. And no wrong is done to anyone. Churches and preachers refer the whole matter of assignment to entirely disinterested parties, and having stated as fully as they wish the desirable adjustment from their point of view, abide by the decision of the "appointing power." And the men who occupy that responsible position, representing the Churches on the one hand and the pastors on the other, having no motive but the good of the Church as a whole, are made secure in their own position so that there is no political or personal interest of their own to be taken into account as they appoint preachers in charge of the Churches throughout Methodism. The wisdom of the system and the security of pastors and Churches depend upon the absolute freedom of the appointing power from all personal solicitude as to its own security from political intrigue and ambition.

One of the most interesting studies in ecclesiastical economy is to be found in our own Church. It is indeed a wonderful system that in the course of twenty years finds no Church for a single Sunday without a pastor and no preacher without a pastorate. An annual conference is in session. Here are three hundred preachers. They represent three hundred Churches or "circuits." Every one of these Churches is officially represented. To every one will be sent for the very next Sunday after the adjournment of the conference a pastor for the ensuing year. It is a wonderful illustration of economy. Every Church has its pastor every Sunday and every pastor has his Church. There is no waste. Misadjustments there may be;

but readjustments are easily possible. And it is often the case that the man thought by the Church to be the "wrong man for us" turns out to be the very man that Church needed. But I am commenting upon ecclesiastical economy whereas the reader expects my "autobiography." And there may be more of biographical revelation than of ecclesiastical comment in these lines. Suppose we do not emphasize this at this time.

I was sent from Galena to Rockford. Every community is representative of some feature of civilization. In Mount Morris I was in the atmosphere of Maryland with a touch of New England. In Galena I found a good deal of old England and of Illinois. In Rockford chiefly New England with the New Illinois – the Yankee element at its best, filled with the enterprise, breadth, and sociability of the later and larger West. Court-street Church was at the time I became acquainted with it full of energy and ready to sustain the pastor in any and everything he recommended. Our Palestine Class was full of enthusiasm, and as I was for the first year of my service in Court-street preparing for a long-cherished scheme of mine – to visit Europe and the Holy Land, the class entered most heartily into its Saturday afternoon studies feeling that as their teacher was soon to visit that region it was in a sense their own opportunity. And right heartily they entered into the studies prescribed and it added to the pleasure of my trip later on to know that they were so enthusiastic over the pilgrimage of their friend and pastor to Paris, Rome, Athens, and Jerusalem.

One of the delightful incidents of my first year in Rockford was the acquaintance formed with Mr. Robert H. Tinker, who was to be my fellow traveler in Europe. He was private secretary to Mrs. Manney of Rockford, the widow of a great manufacturer and living in a palatial home near the shore of the Rock River. One day, after the fact of my projected tour had been announced, Mrs. Manney's carriage drove up to the door of the home in which Mrs. Vincent and I were living, and in the course of the conversation between Mrs. Manney, Mrs. Vincent, Mr. Tinker, and myself, Mr. Tinker asked if the report were true that I purposed to go to Europe. Learning that I expected to go he asked if I had any traveling companion. Then he asked if I cared for a fellow pilgrim. Of course, I assured him that I greatly desired one. Promptly he said: "I shall go with you." This was news to the good lady whose secretary he was. But Rob had made up his mind and a few weeks later we started.

There was one feature of the first trip to Europe which I have not widely advertised. Rob, and I met in New York and went to make inquiries about routes and steamers. When we had selected the line and ship Rob said, "Now do you choose a good state room and get your ticket for it. I intend," he added, "to go by steerage." This astonished and distressed me. I said, "I never in my life went by any other way than the first class." He answered, "I should not think of having *you* go in that economical way." I replied that "when men travel together, they *must* go in the same class," and so we made our first trip by steerage. We saved money by it. And going eastward it was not like a trip with emigrants from the other side of the Atlantic. The ship was clean. The passengers were respectable foreigners who had been in the United States for several years. And there were ministers, school-teachers, students, and business men who wanted to travel as cheaply as possible. The ventilation was perfect, much better than in most of the first-class cabins and staterooms of that day. The fare was good; and an extra shilling now and then secured some little luxury not on the bill of fare in the "class" we patronized. But it was a good thing when at the end of about fourteen days we landed at Queenstown, took a first-class room in a good hotel and ate and slept and rested and rejoiced that we were again on *terra firma*. I never really regretted that steerage trip. But crossing the Atlantic seventeen times after that I always allowed the steerage experience to be nothing but a memory.

How good the food in a clean Irish hotel! How sweet the bread and the butter, although saltless! How fresh and palatable it was! And the "rolls," and the fresh eggs, and the tea, ah, what tea they do serve both in Ireland and England! Then came two weeks of foot-travel in the fine air and over the smooth roads and among the lakes and mountains of Ireland. We visited Killarney and went through town and country all the way to the extreme north. We saw and took notes. We chatted with the cordial natives and my good friend and fellow traveler can tell to this day, and in the brogue of the natives, the sharp things they said and the curious questions they asked about our own land beyond the seas. Great days they were those first days beyond the seas!

This is not the place nor have we the time to give the details of our journey in Ireland and Scotland and good old conservative England. We were treated cordially by all classes of people. I preached very often in Irish, Scotch, and English pulpits, and met scores of dear people who loved the Christ we worshiped, believed in the national freedom we represented, and had friends on our side of the sea in whom they were interested.

It is not possible just here and now to report the whole of that first and memorable journey, extending through nearly or quite a year, by which I became acquainted with the principal countries and peoples of Europe and prepared the way for later journeys and finally for a four years' residence in Switzerland as bishop of the Methodist Episcopal Church. Of that quadrennium I may speak a little later in this series of reminiscences. The most interesting part of my foreign tour of 1862-63 was my first visit to Egypt, Palestine, Athens, and Asia Minor. Of this let me write a little later.

I have no words by which adequately to express the interest and profit added to my first journey to Europe by my charming traveling companion, Mr. Tinker. The "wanderlust" was warm within him. Born in the Sandwich Islands, the son of a Presbyterian clergyman, brought in his early childhood to America, fond of out-of-door life, full of humor, with a keen sense of the ludicrous, courageous and venturesome, patient and genial always, with no moods of depression and withal sympathetic, my traveling companion "Rob" was a treasure to be prized at the time and to be remembered with tenderest affection through all the years. It was a matter of regret that he could not accompany me to the land of Egypt and the pilgrimage through Palestine. "Rob" had the artist's gift as well, and his letters home were a treasure, enriching as he could the pages of his record with pictorial illustrations which gave them double charm.

It was also on this my first trip to Europe that a good providence gave me as a fellow traveler and Christian companion and counselor a Baptist minister, a fine scholar, an expert and merciless critic and withal a really spiritually minded and stimulating associate. I refer to my intimate friend, Rev. Dr. William Cleaver Wilkinson. The Chautauquans, especially those connected with the "C. L. S. C." in its earlier years, will recall the interesting, stimulating, and illuminating books of Dr. Wilkinson – the volumes in which the "college student's outlook" in Greek, Latin, German, and French literature was made delightfully clear and inspiring. I have had many friends, some of them over-careful as literary men and scholars, not to – and I leave the sentence unfinished. But Dr. Wilkinson was always frank, outspoken, "critical," sometimes "severe." And more than anyone can know I am indebted to him for literary, pedagogical, and spiritual ministries, the full value and appreciation of which I cannot express in words.

## CHAPTER 19

# The Autobiography of Bishop Vincent

# Sixteenth Paper[1]

*August 3, 1910*

From Court-street Church, Rockford, I was, at the conference of 1864 sent to Trinity Church, Chicago, then located on the corner of Indiana Avenue and Twenty-first Street. There was a small and uncomfortable brick parsonage back of the old (then comparatively new) Trinity Church. It was a new enterprise with few members but gave promise of a good future. Among its members were the families of the substantial and well-to-do Brother Wheeler and Dr. Thomas M. Eddy, then editor of the *NORTHWESTERN CHRISTIAN ADVOCATE*. The people of the Church were not very enthusiastic, but it was substantial in its "make-up" and aspired to be accounted, as it generally was, "a Church of the better class of people" (whatever that meant) and I was accounted honored in being appointed as the pastor. Of a few little drawbacks in the situation, I need say nothing now. I was there but a year and it was my last pastorate. The people treated me cordially, but it was not Joliet, Mount Morris, Rockford, or Galena. There were few children in the congregation.

1. *Northwestern Christian Advocate,* Vol. 58, No. 31, pages 10 and 20.

The "Palestine Class" was not possible, although I tried to organize such a Saturday afternoon ministry which had proved such a success in every other parish to which I had been appointed from Irvington in New Jersey to Court-street, Rockford, in Illinois. My congregation at Trinity was small, well dressed, kind, and attentive. I tried to do my best. But my best did not build up much more of a congregation than I found there when I first left Rockford.

The Church and Sunday School workers outside of Methodism welcomed me most heartily and I found very soon an opening under union auspices for a movement which turned out to be far more radical, popular, and successful than at first I dreamed of as at all practicable. And it was there in 1865 that the Sunday School movement began its development in Chicago which resulted in several unfoldings which are to-day well and widely known. It began in Chicago at that time in a series of special addresses, lectures, model lessons, institute sessions, and the establishment of a magazine and the institution of the "Lesson Leaf" system of lessons which afterward became general, national, and international. In the appendix "H," page 339, of "The Modern Sunday School," published by the Methodist Book Concern, may be found a copy of the first "Lesson Leaf" of the modern series now scattered weekly or monthly over the Christian world. And it is a matter of personal gratification and of humble thankfulness to the Divine Spirit that this first leaf anticipated so much in method and principle that has since then followed. Through the success of that leaf and the new Sunday School magazine (the *Sunday School Quarterly*) and then the monthly that followed, the whole modern Sunday School lesson system was developed.

While the Methodist Episcopal Sunday School Union at New York called me to that city to serve as general agent of the union under the supervision of the corresponding secretary, Dr.

Daniel Wise, the Chicago movement, through the enterprise and energy of B. F. Jacobs and the brilliant editorial genius of Edward Eggleston was made a great success.[2] The example of the Chicago scheme and of the new Methodist movement in New York gave a fresh impulse to the entire Sunday School world, and what with the conventions, institutes, normal classes, the new publications of all the denominations and unions[,] the fresh suggestions before institutes and conventions – the Sunday School work loomed large before the entire Church. The strong men – biblical scholars and ecclesiastical leaders who had never before thought much about the Sunday School as of really great importance – began to appreciate its possibilities as an educational agency for the local Church the world over.

It was chiefly through the agency and the persistency of B. F. Jacobs of Chicago that this large, beneficent, and really Christian union movement was consummated. Many who had faith in its value doubted its practicability. Jacobs was a born leader, a battery of enthusiasm, a most devout soul, as generous as he was courageous, and he pushed the plan of national uniformity with persistency.

An important factor in the general Sunday School movement of the early sixties was the "Sunday School Institute" and "Normal Class" device by which the entire Church was awakened to the necessity of higher standards of attainment and of methods educational among the rank and file of the Sunday School teachers and officers of the Churches. If the Sunday School be nothing more than a voluntary society, outside and independent of the Church, a society for pious appeals to little children, especially those who lack home care and counsel, it can never become the real nursery

2. Edward Eggleston (1837-1902), Methodist minister, historian, and novelist.

of the Church. Nor can it (under this limited theory) command the respect of adolescence nor the confidence of thoughtful, cultivated Church members. If in any sense a "school" it must be a *school*. It must have a strong and solid system pedagogic underneath it. The pastor must put not only his heart but his brains into it. He must keep his hands of authority upon it. He must secure the intelligent and energetic cooperation of the most scholarly women and men in his congregation to go to it, to teach in it, to see that their own children regularly attend, and that at home they make as careful and thorough preparation for its services as they do for the recitations of the regular day school.

It was a firm conviction years ago in this direction that led to the organization of local Sunday School institutes and normal classes for the training of Sunday School teachers and officers to discharge their official duties after a fashion that would command the respect of secular educators. The writer of this article in the early years of his own pastorate wrote these words: "The secular teachers tell the little ones of God in nature; we of God in grace. They conduct them through the outer courts of the cosmos; we lead them beyond the veil into the innermost sanctuary, where God's voice is heard, and where man may commune face to face with him. We must therefore be 'apt to teach.' We are to show ourselves 'approved' – 'workmen that need not to be ashamed, rightly dividing the word of truth.'"[3]

At the Rock River annual conference at Chicago in 1860 the conference committee made appeal in its report for "Teachers' Institutes conducted by our ablest Sunday School educators." April 16 following, at the Galena district convention, a "teachers' institute" was organized having for its object "the increase of

3. 2 Timothy 2:15.

Sunday School interest and efficiency throughout Galena District." Four subdistricts were ordered: Galena, Warren, Freeport, Mount Carroll. It is interesting to-day to read the delightful, published reports of those subdistrict institutes. They were occasions of great enthusiasm. The writer of this record read an essay, November 17, 1864, before the Cook County Sunday School Convention in Chicago on "A Permanent Sunday School Teachers' Institute for the Northwest." And in all these early appeals for higher ideals and more thorough methods ample credit was always given to the earliest and most aggressive movements in the direction of Sunday School teacher training to the early work in this direction by the London Sunday School Union.

In a little volume by the writer of this paper, published by the Methodist Book Room in New York, in 1872, entitled "Sunday School Institutes and Normal Classes" (possibly now out of print) the whole subject of Sunday School teacher training was discussed; and many programs for normal classes and institutes published.

Notwithstanding the efforts of all the foremost Sunday School leaders through the past half century there is still a pressing demand for aggressive work in this direction. Indeed, the demand was never so imperative in view of the development of the whole subject of pedagogy in all the fields of educational effort. Mothers and fathers are beginning to take an interest in the science and art of teaching. The best literature is being distributed widely. Certainly, it behooves the Church in all its departments and denominations to give renewed and most careful attention to the science and the art of teaching in the home, the day school, the press, and especially in the Church.

No, the spiritual energies of grace will not be diminished by this wise emphasis on the scientific processes which are the outgrowth of a careful and conscientious study of the "ways of God" in the intellectual and spiritual kingdom at the heart of which he reigns, and through the processes of which he trains immortal souls for a glorious and immortal destiny. In the rapturous and triumphant songs of heaven "grace" and "love" are not allowed to suppress praise and thanksgiving for "knowledge" and "wisdom."

Dr. William E. Channing of New England, in an address before an educational association in 1837, pleaded for an institute for the training of secular teachers. In 1839 Dr. Barnard[4] held such an institute in Hartford, Conn.

* * *

On Wednesday, April 17, 1861, at Freeport, Ill., a teacher's institute was attempted in the interest of Sunday School officers and teachers. And provision was then and there made for "a permanent Sunday School teachers' institute under the auspices of the Galena District of the Rock River annual conference." A constitution was adopted, the district divided into four subdistricts. Several institutes were held that year. The exercises consisted of devotional services, scripture studies (historical and doctrinal) conducted, class drills and lectures – illustrations given, specimens of the teaching process presented, and criticisms of the frankest type offered. The writer of these lines in November 1861, issued a circular explaining the institute, its object, possible methods, with a list of over forty topics for essays and discussions, which circular was widely copied by the religious press.

In June of 1861 a Detroit Methodist Episcopal Sunday School institute was held in Detroit, Rev. M. Hickey, president. This institute was kept for many years. Possibly it is still in existence.

4. American education reformer Henry Barnard (1811 – 1900). Barnard was an activist on behalf of public schools and teacher training.

After this inauguration the Sunday School institute and normal classwork was carried on widely and with great success. Dr. D. P. Kidder[5] in charge of years of the Sunday School department of the Methodist Episcopal Church, as early as 1847 made a plea for "Normal Sabbath School instruction." The London Sunday School Union in 1859 instituted a Sunday School normal class.

* * *

There is no end to the list of reasons for emphasizing in our own times the great work of training the laity of the Church in the principles and methods of the highest pedagogy. Home, as it is the first, is the most important of all schools. Fathers and mothers should study with greatest care the whole field of education, beginning with the too little appreciated prenatal problems, beginning in the earliest weeks of the child's life to apply the principles of a true psychology and pedagogy to the training of the young animal that is to be bane or blessing to society.

This is a subject which the pulpit can well afford to discuss, and which it should discuss even if the congregation have reason to imagine that the parsonage itself would do well to consider these problems. It is a question of far more importance than any "revival," past, projected, or possible. It supplements the ministries of the pulpit and the pastoral visitation. It calls for the wide distribution of the strongest tracts that have been written on both sides of the sea. It should be deemed urgent enough to ensure the holding of mothers' meetings, fathers' councils, local conventions of both teachers and parents. It would be a good subject for a series of vigorous articles in the weekly or daily press. It should

5. MEC theologian Daniel Parish Kidder (1815 – 1891) was a writer and missionary to Brazil.

especially be a theme for conventions of day school teachers. A Church prayer meeting could well afford to make it a standing theme for two evenings every spring and two more every autumn. The pastor might well invite the wisest day school teacher of the community to speak in the pulpit twice a year on the relations of the home and the secular school. The rich literature now being produced covering the wide range of education might be circulated. If the day school teachers could provide a quarterly question department for the local press it would provoke thought among parents and increase their sense of responsibility.

* * *

No, this is no argument against the democratic idea of education in the public school. Nor is it possible to draw from our words of caution an argument in favor of the parochial school – which is as un-American as it is cowardly. When the home and the Church do their duty there is no possible harm from a secular school system. If our ecclesiastical system – Methodist, Mormon, Papist, or Presbyterian – be afraid of genuine and thorough education, the education of our youth in history, science, political economy, the ability to think and to reason and to speak out boldly their opinions, then it may be well to shut them up in parochial schools and train them to challenge the right of American citizens to think for themselves. But in our age and in our land we need to make home the first school of habit, or reverence, of manners, of social good-will, of the history of the [human] race and its gradual developments, of the civilizations under which the largest measure of popular education has been encouraged and the freedom of the individual most safely and effectively secured. If under such training congregationalism or Methodism has to go to the ground and "bite the dust," the sooner the better. My God founded it. God protects it. And through its power, and the civilization it develops I am at liberty to worship God according to the dictates of my own conscience. And if any religious theory which I hold interferes with my loyalty to the Constitution of the United States, I have very good reason for revising my opinions, or at least for going to some other country where other people will do my thinking for me.

Every Church should give attention to the training of its youth to be loyal and intelligent citizens, to be generous in judging others, to study the history of civilization, and to ascertain under what system the largest liberty is guaranteed to the individual, the most intelligent loyalty to the government at the same time guaranteed, and the security and happiness of the greatest number of citizens ensured. No party and no organization, social or political, should be encouraged the mission of which is to bring the people under the rule of a society, party, sect, or fraternity hostile to the most thorough education of the individual and his fullest enjoyment of all the advantages of education, together with the absolute right to express his opinion by voice or vote, subject always to the Constitution of the nation under which he lives.

CHAPTER 20

# The Autobiography of Bishop Vincent

## Seventeenth Paper[1]

---

*August 10, 1910*

From my tour of Europe and Palestine I returned to old Court-street Church in Rockford and had the great privilege of serving that dear people another year. The Palestine pupils gave me a most cordial welcome. And I think the class was greatly improved by the opportunities its leader had enjoyed of traveling through the countries connected with the great Textbook – especially Italy, Greece, Egypt, and Palestine. The members of the class felt that it was an advantage to have as teacher one who had himself seen the Nile, the Red Sea, the Mediterranean, the Dead Sea, and the Jordan, and who had traveled from Joppa to Jerusalem, climbed Olivet, and gone from Hebron in the South to Hermon and Lebanon and Damascus in the North. And yet it is literally true that many people who have never "been abroad" do know a deal more about Europe and the country along the eastern shores of the Mediterranean than many travelers who have gone from point to point by steam or carriage, on horseback or on foot, keeping their eyes open and yet easily overlooking or forgetting

1. *Northwestern Christian Advocate*, Vol. 58, No. 32, pages 11-12.

what the diligent and eager reader at home holds in his memory and sees through his imagination, not needing what the traveler often has to do – looking up his own journal to make sure that he "really did go to that place."

The enthusiasm of my old Palestine pupils suggests a point that I may as well make here as anywhere else in my story. The possibilities of the pastorate, on its educational side, are not strongly enough impressed upon candidates for the ministry by the theological teachers. A pastor is in reality a theological seminary president, and it is his business to train all of his people in the knowledge of Bible history, geography, ancient manners and customs, and, far more than this, to put greater stress on the possibilities and the consequent responsibilities of the laity in the whole matter of education – secular and sacred. This field of influence and active endeavor is not limited to the preachers, pastors, and Sunday School teachers. In fact, the earliest and most important of all teachers are the parents. And if normal training of the most thorough type is anywhere needed it is at home, that parents may cooperate with the best teachers, secular and religious, in making really good and diligent students of their children, thus anticipating and supplementing the best public and Sunday School work. Parents should become familiar with and skillful in applying every pedagogic principle that the pulpit and the day school employ in the great work of education. The most urgent demand of the times is home teaching by intelligent, studious, and consecrated parents. When a plain, unlettered mother induces her boy to tell her what he is expecting to tell his teacher that day, she may not be able to correct any of his mistakes, but he will soon make fewer mistakes because of the discipline gained by his sincere endeavor. The greatest need in this age is not pulpit but home, not oratory but pedagogy, not aesthetic Church ministries but the authority and example of vigorous, personal, Christian character – first of all and always in father and mother. And here the pastor has heavy responsibility.

There are before me as I write memoranda made in 1861, and even earlier than that, concerning my own Sunday School, its teachers and their pupils, which show how early and strong were the emphasis on the cooperation of the home, the Church, and the Sunday School, and how fully was recognized the necessity of taking into the Sunday School all the most advanced methods of the public school. In our local Church *Bulletin,* I find that every class had its name and motto: the name of every pupil was published in the *Annual*. There, too, was the "choral circle" for training in sacred music that "all might acquire the art of singing with ease, spirit, and effect." Even in those early days the Sunday School was recognized as an organic part of the Church, a supplement to the home, and was never accounted a substitute for the "public service."

In the number of my Church *Annual* for 1862 I find a "Plan of Study for the Year." Here, too, are "golden texts" for the whole year. Here is a "Missionary Plan for the School for 1862," and here a "List of the Members of the Court-street Sunday School now in the Army." Among these were a former superintendent, three teachers, and six scholars. That old organization was an enterprising, progressive, enthusiastic, well-organized, well-officered, and well-directed Sunday School. The best of this later age will present no nobler ideals than those embodied in the plans of the Court-street Methodist Episcopal Sunday School in Rockford, Ill., in 1862-63.

Of course, we dream of and hope for better things in some early to-morrow when the ideals of that time will be realized, the Sunday School more closely wedded to the Church, the supplemental week-day work of the Church more thoroughly pastoral and effective, the educational standards higher, the teachers better trained for their work of subpastoral service, and the ethical and spiritual ministries of the institution made more sane, steady, truly scientific, and both ethically and spiritually more effective.

If in my work as a "Sunday School specialist" I made one emphasis stronger than another it was in the following: Home first, home second, home third. The Sunday School must be an extension of the home. The two must cooperate. The three institutions must always aim to go together: Home, Church, Sunday School. The three are one. Or may we say: The Church has two departments; home and Sunday School. Both are auxiliary to the Church, which is the divinely organized agency in the world for the salvation of the world. The Church itself is a school. The public service is a form of both home and school. All Church members are disciples. The one text-book is the Holy Bible. Its corps of instructors is made up of parents, pastors, class leaders, Sunday School officers and teachers. Blessed is the Church organized, officered, and ordered on this comprehensive and biblical theory. It reproduces the New Testament methods. It proclaims the gospel to the [human] race. It recognizes the home as the ideal of the Church. It transforms the Church into a garden of grace, a gateway into the celestial fellowships. And as through the pulpit it proclaims and defends the truth, through the home it illustrates the truth and through the school it directly applies that truth to the individual and builds up unit after unit in the holy faith that Christ established on the earth.

While discussing the work of the Sunday School let me appeal for a stronger emphasis upon the effort of the teacher in behalf of the individual pupil. It is the power of personal effort and of personality upon personality that really counts in religious work, especially in Sunday School work. The musical ministry is inspiring. The concert responses when "the whole school" is appealed to for "a hearty, rousing, simultaneous answer" are helpful in the development of enthusiasm. Everybody is awake. The "whole school" shouts it out, or sings "to take the roof off" as the magnetic leader suggests. The *esprit de corps* is developed. Everybody is aroused. "A great school is ours" says the well-pleased pastor as he congratulates the superintendent.

But all this may be to the last degree superficial. It may foster an enthusiasm precisely the reverse of the "real need" of that school. The value of the Church school, which we call the Sunday School, is in the personal effect of the general and individual work on the individual pupil, and that not in class or school enthusiasm but in personal conviction of truth as it applies to the unit – the separate, responsible person whom we call a "scholar." And the main aim is not to make him an enthusiastic member of "our school," but to cause him to know and to feel the reality of his responsibility to God.

The modern Sunday School needs "more religion" in it; a more intelligent, personal conviction as to the relation of the young soul to God; a more earnest desire on the part of the teacher to bring this personality to a sense of sin, responsibility, surrender, faith in the reality of the lessons we study, and the "golden texts" we commit to memory. We need more seriousness, more actual earnestness on the part of teacher and taught. The best Sunday School class work is work that sends the child, the adult, and especially the adolescent away from the Sunday School session with earnest thoughts, desires, and resolves in his (or her) young soul. Good cheer, the social spirit, a touch of spontaneous enthusiasm in the life and work and fellowships of the school – all this is legitimate, but the main end of Sunday School life and effort is to convince the pupil of religious obligation, his personal obligation to God. And when this end is reached and the Sunday School becomes a true believer in and follower of Christ the real mission of the Sunday School begins which is to bring up and to build up that new disciple in the service of society as a believer in and an earnest follower of Christ.

* * *

It is just here that I want to confess that my work in the Church and as a pastor lacked what, if I had opportunity to try it all over again, I should more earnestly seek and emphasize: A stronger and more positive emphasis on the subjective life; an intelligent emphasis on the present inward witness of the divine Spirit, as a possibility for every believer. The faith in the doctrines which this involves I have always had. But the *emphasis* I did not always make as every pastor and preacher should. This does not involve and imply, as some fancy, a somber and melancholy religion that withdraws from all social life and that depreciates a positive emphasis on culture, on science, on art, on sane recreative life, etc. I do not for a moment believe in a religion that is always engaged in introspection, and that is too serious to enjoy good neighborship and the play of humor. But there is a life that finds delight in the deeper, richer, stronger realities of faith, in prayer, public and private, in devotional reading, in simple, genuine, unaffected, spontaneous conversation on "the ways of God with the believing soul." This sane and beautiful inner life finds pleasure in the study of Christian biography, in the careful and critical study of present social conditions and needs. It delights in all modern forms of Christian philanthropy, but it makes sure that all the while it "has an understanding with God," resting in him while it seeks in all wise ways to serve man. It looks forward with delight to the eternal life but finds equal pleasure in present service not only in aiding individuals who need sympathy and help but in equally earnest efforts for the improvement of a present civilization, never forgetting the responsibilities of the ballot box and the political rostrum through their faith in the felicities of the heaven that lies beyond the valley of death.

The Sunday School needs stronger faith in the fact of personal responsibility for the life within – the personal witness of acceptance with God. A child may have it. And such training and such subjective experience are the surest protection of our youth from the really dangerous elements of modern social life. Our young people should be so trained as to have a positive personal conviction of the reality of the spiritual kingdom, their relation to it, and the possibilities of harmonizing all its requirements with everything worth while [sic] in the fields of social life, recreation, and a "good time," the best of good times that life has to offer. In this line of instruction lie the protecting influences which it is the business of the Church to provide for all the youths under her care.

## CHAPTER 21

# The Autobiography of Bishop Vincent

# Eighteenth Paper[2]

***August 17, 1910***

My assignment in the fall of 1864 to the pastorate of Trinity Church, Chicago, was the first step toward a field of service outside of the pastorate. Trinity was a new enterprise at the corner of Indiana Avenue and Twenty-first Street. It was not in any sense, as was Court-street, Rockford, a "people's Church." It was a small, unpretentious stone building with a congregation having more wealth than numbers, more conservatism than enthusiasm, and I thought at the time more "social" aspiration than evangelistic fervor. There were very few children and youth in the congregation. It was a quiet, conservative, well-to-do group of believers with little enthusiasm about anything – pleasant, hospitable, kind-hearted folks, greeting each other and the pastor as they chanced to meet with cheerful faces and as hearty handshakes as the busy Chicagoans of that time had to offer.

I soon found that there was no chance in Trinity for a Palestine class, nor for a normal class, nor had I gifts as an attractive "pulpit orator," nor did I care much (indeed not enough) for "parlor life." Trinity was unlike anything I had ever known in Church life. It was

2. *Northwestern Christian Advocate,* Vol. 58, No. 33, pages 11 and 23.

not an "ice house." It was indeed in every sense a "nice house," and many pastors I have since known would have rejoiced in the opportunities it opened. The people were very cordial. The weakness of the Church was neither "fashion" nor "social ambition." It was really more in danger from "apathy." A lovely, kind, contented, cordial people they all were. They had comfortable homes and loved to be at home. In a sense they were hospitable, and really wanted and tried to "encourage" the pastor and to be "interested in the Church."

The situation at Trinity gave me time and inclination to respond to the cordial greetings and fellowships of the "downtown" Young Men's Christian Association and "Sunday School Union" people. While I did not for a night nor an hour neglect my own ecclesiastical flock and family, I did find a hearty response to my enthusiasm in Bible and Sunday School work in the men like Jacobs and Moody and other "union"-loving disciples. I was faithful in pastoral visitation. I tried to organize in Trinity a "Palestine class," but in vain. There were few children in Trinity. And "Saturday is such a busy day," they said.

Association with the downtown workers and their enthusiastic response to my suggestions for an "advance" in Sunday School lines led to the organization of a movement out of which came a new Sunday School magazine, the first *Lesson Leaf* of these later days, and that was the initial development of the great lesson system which to-day has such a hold on the Christian world on both hemispheres.

From my father I had inherited Sunday School enthusiasm. He had been a Sunday School worker and superintendent from my earliest recollection. In my pastorates in 1852-56, in New Jersey, and later in Joliet, Mount Morris, Galena, and Rockford, Ill., I had given especial attention to Bible study through Bible classes, normal classes, Sunday School institutes, and the "Palestine class," and when I was appointed to Trinity in the "sixties" I found myself providentially prepared for a Sunday School movement that emphasized teacher training and a new system of uniform and graded Sunday School teaching which has already girdled the globe. It was this system to which the gifted Edward Eggleston afterward consecrated his genius for some time before his death and which through the initiative and enthusiastic persistency of Jacobs became national. And later on, the full fruitage of the movement has been gathered in the great world-wide "International Lesson System." To this last form of development I gave all of my personal effort and enthusiasm.

The success of the lesson leaf and the institute movement led all the denominations to put more emphasis upon Bible study. In every Church a new zeal was manifest. The "National Lesson Committee" was organized. Churches the world over were enlisted, and now for years Protestant Christendom has been unified to a surprising degree in the study of the Word of God.

The attention which I gave to this kind of work made it necessary for me, if I continued to develop it, to retire from the pastorate. This was a difficult thing for me to do. In yielding first to the pressure of the situation and later to the call of my Church, I resolved that in giving myself to this as a specialty I should never allow myself to neglect theological studies and the peaching of the gospel, seeking to avoid the peril to which a "specialty" exposes the preacher of the Word. At the call of Dr. Wise and the Sunday School Board of the Church, I first became the agent of the union and was later on elected corresponding secretary of the Sunday School Union and editor of its publications until elected to the episcopacy in 1888.

While always active in cooperative Christian work in which all the denominations were enlisted, I have been an advocate of the separate forms of the Church known as "denominations." The unity of a village or town does not require all the families of the place to live under one roof and to take their meals at a common table. The highest form of Christian union is found in the "denominational" system. It is well to have many Churches with different forms of government, methods of aggressive, educational, and missionary effort in "societies" which utilize the enterprise and services of many men and women.

The "denominations" of Christianity are a great benefit to the Church, to society, and to the state, if effective cooperative work in a wide field is desirable. It is better than if there were but one society, one set of officers, and one administrative center. People differ. Civilizations differ. Policies must differ. It is better for a score of reasons. It is better for the city or town to be made up of families living in separate houses rather than in one huge hotel, eating in one dining-room, sleeping under the same roof. Individuality is as important as general and organic unity. An individuality is almost sure to be weakened when pressure must be brought to secure the quiet of concurrence, the sacrifice of opinion and preference, "sweet harmony" for unbroken and unbreakable oneness! Thus, truth must be suppressed for the sake of unity. Discussion has from the very outset the disadvantage of this dominating demand for unity, *unity*, UNITY! A discussion without a chance at experimentation is not worth much.

The various denominations draw the lines sharply, and that not for "rivalry" but for instruction and scientific experimentation. The members of each body discuss among themselves as they prepare their own literature and present to all classes of people their reasons for existence. The people, thus separately housed, provide a literature that sets forth their history and emphasis. Representatives of a denomination write and publish, and others read and investigate, and many a time people who *say* nothing emphasize or modify their own views through the calm, clear, earnest, vigorous "putting" of "the other side" by its representatives.

The division, the possibility of frank discussion, the actual scientific experimentation – all these are fruits of the denominational development of Protestant Christendom. Partisanship, selfish rivalry, personal ambitions, real estate enterprises, "withdrawals" from older Churches, etc., may create temporary conflict, and now and then un-Christian conditions, but politics will do that, and local debating societies may do that. But truth is extended.

"It is too bad," said a dear old lady in the country, when a debating society was organized and which she was persuaded to attend, "it is too bad to set folks against each other like that – neighbors, too. I don't believe that the Nelson family will ever allow one of their children to speak to one of the Smiths after that awful quarrel of the two boys at the debate last night." But, just then, the old lady, looking out of the window, saw the Nelson boy and the Smith boy driving by in the Smith buggy, both fellows roaring with laughter, and she said, "Well, that beats me!"

There is a difference that makes for unity. A great truth is greater when it has been looked at from two, three, or more sides. Denominationalism makes for discussion and practical social experimentation, and thus contributes to a unity that is worth while, and to a wider and more varied opportunity to know and to appreciate the relative value of emphasis, theological and ecclesiastical. When we decide that all citizens of a town or city must live in one colossal hotel and under one roof of vast acreage in order to good neighborship and perfect cooperation, we may attempt to bring everybody into "one visible Church" and carefully suppress discussion that we have "unity." But such "unity" is not "Christian unity."

CHAPTER 22

# The Autobiography of Bishop Vincent

# Nineteenth Paper[1]

***August 24, 1910***

Many years before the suggestion of the Epworth League, an organization was proposed and effected for the training of our young and more aggressive people to give them a higher appreciation of our denominational mission and a better knowledge of the relations of the earlier Methodism to the broader and larger life of consecrated culture.

Inasmuch as the scheme was conceived in my own study in New Jersey and while I was officially at the head of the Sunday School department of the Methodist Episcopal Church, it was of course a matter of regret to me that it was deemed necessary to abandon the name of the "Oxford League" in order to effect a compromise with those who had identified themselves with other alliances, clubs, societies not under the direction and control of our own Church. It is not possible to tell the story of my personal and official life and leave out what I deem one of the most important of the devices conceived and proposed in the interest of the youth of Methodism.

1. *Northwestern Christian Advocate*, Vol. 58, No. 34, pages 11 and 26.

Although already elsewhere referred to in these reminiscences I must again and more fully report the ideas and ideals of the Oxford League, the chief design of which was to connect in the thought of our young Methodists the relation in the beginning of what is "Methodism," of the Methodist movement to the life and ideals of the university. Modern Methodism began not in the gutter, not in the slums, but in the university and in the most delightful homes of England. It did not "climb up." It began its blessed work by "going down." The earliest Methodists were college men. They were believers, as John Wesley was, in the broadest and most thorough education.

Go to Oxford for the story of the founding of the modern movement in the Church which we call Methodism. Find it in the group of students – serious fellows – who, under the shadow of the university, studied the holy gospels in the original language and then went forth as faithful missioners to visit the poor, the sick, the prisoners, and all who needed light and sympathy and service. The beginning of Methodism – the New Testament type of service – was not in the jail but in the college class room, not among the ignorant and besotted but among university students and scholars. You find it in the university chamber where a group of ambitious and eager students surrounded a table for the study of the New Testament in the original Greek, and where, as the light of the Holy Word fell upon them, they lifted their souls in prayer for the divine grace. And from this holy chamber they went out to visit the poor, the neglected, the vicious people of the town. It was there and then that modern Methodism began.

The Oxford League I recommend to the young Methodists of this century is a memorial and a reproduction of that original: our most earnest and intelligent young people convened as students, representatives of our worthiest families, ambitious young people who as thoughtful students in the school of Christ are eager to grow in knowledge, in grace, and in skill as workers together with Christ. It is a league of people (chiefly young people) with high ideals of culture and character and of truly refined social life, intent in giving all the best that is in them to the service of the race.

Of course, the Epworth League has its memories and its historical associations as it recalls the rectory of Epworth with its eccentric old rector, Samuel Wesley, and the real "head" of the family, Susannah Wesley, with her big family, and the wise policies she adopted in training and regulating as she did both husband and children. It is all very interesting and unique, a chapter full of eccentricities, full of charm; but to me the college group of students, bringing with them to Oxford the influence of a faithful mother, and gathering week after week under the noble towers of the venerable university to search the Scriptures and to ask for wiser and better ways of living and of working – all this is a nobler, richer, and more suggestive picture for our young Methodists of the age we are living in, and is likely to inspire with the noblest ideals far beyond anything the Epworth rectory may give us. "Epworth" stands for one thing, "Oxford" for all that Epworth suggests and a great deal more.

The Oxford League made all the emphasis I have above described: the emphasis on the fact that modern Methodism originated in a university; that it did not spring from depths of ignorance and superstition; that it was not a conception of ignorant people but that it came to us from university halls and from the strong, wise, and earnest Christian home, and that, thus prepared, it went forth reaching up and reaching down to capture society through the family and the college and in the interest of a genuine, enlightened, refined, and aggressive social, educational, and spiritual life.

Why then may we not have a development of the old Oxford dream in connection with the Epworth organization – an Oxford Club of the Epworth League or the Epworth League of the Oxford Club, emphasizing the early university alliances of the modern Methodist movement? This reminder of our early ecclesiastical relation to the higher education, and the fact that our fathers and founders were university men, would not weaken the hold of Methodism upon the increasing multitudes of scholars which the colleges and universities of the age are sending out into every circle of our modern society. Consider the following plan:

1. We (here insert names) agree to form an Oxford Club for the study of the facts concerning the original so-called "Holy Club" at Oxford University in England, in which the Wesley brothers were especially interested.
2. The club once organized shall devote itself first of all to the reading of all accessible records concerning that club, as found in biographies and other historical memoranda.
3. The club shall aim to promote a higher appreciation among its members of a true scholarship as a factor in religious and Church life, answering thoroughly the superficial and false idea that high scholarship is hostile to deep and fervent piety.
4. The club shall urge upon its members and all the young people it may be able to influence, to take, if at all possible, a "college course of study," and so examine carefully the whole subject as to be able to make it appear that a full college education is a much easier matter than is usually supposed, and that "Where there's a will there's a way."
5. The club shall encourage all its members who have not, and who conclude that they cannot, enjoy the advantage of a regular

college education, to at least pursue courses of reading at home which shall give them the broader outlook of the scholar.

6. The club shall make a specialty of Church history, and especially of Christian biography.
7. The club shall provide an annual course of lectures on every phase of Church life, putting especial emphasis on the work of social reform and philanthropic ministry in every possible form, emphasizing especially the lives of the great world philanthropists.

It will be an easy thing to keep the Epworth League organization intact and to increase its power and popularity by the emphasis upon the Oxford Club that takes us all back to the splendid movement that turned the Epworth rectory and the Oxford university into a joint agency for the increase of a true home influence, a noble scholarship, and a fervent piety, all of them expressing themselves in the development of the noblest type of philanthropy that the world has ever known.

While it is true that no kind or quantity of what is called "culture" can ever "save" a soul, it is also true that "knowledge is power," and that, other things being equal, the cultivated, scholarly man or woman of broad horizon, and enriched by knowledge of varied fields of human learning, can be far more useful in our age and under our American civilization than an ignorant and resourceless saint. I well understand that wrinkle of challenge on the reader's brow. And I hear the names you repeat in your mind: Moody, Bramwell, Bunyan, Burns, etc., and scores of plain, unlettered men in all the fields of reform, literature, religion, etc.

And I am sure you remember how much profound thought and wise invention and hours of concentrated attention these men employed as the years went on; how closely and with what time-forgetting concentration they thought and thought and thought, dropping into profound depths and rising to lofty heights, the powers of their souls developing at every effort and the marvelous mastery they gained, and the treasure of truth they contributed to the world's civilization.

Let us train our youth to appreciate the wealth of learning and the wonders of achievement possible to them if they are willing to pay the price by persistency in concentration. Let the Oxford ideal as it grows in our thought in the study of the early development of Methodism, lead us as ministers, teachers, and parents to inspire all the young people (and older folk as well) whom we can influence, to make the Church, the home, and the everyday life opportunities for the enlargement, enrichment, and ennoblement of personality – for the good of the race and for the glory of God. A higher scholarship fully consecrated to God is the demand of the day. Let us stand and live and plead for it as the noblest consummation of the civilization – the Christian civilization – under which we live and thrive and rejoice.

CHAPTER 23

# The Autobiography of Bishop Vincent

## Twentieth Paper[1]

---

*August 31, 1910*

As pastor I sought to make this emphasis: The Church is a "school" – a group of "disciples" under training, and the pastor is a "teacher." He should teach in all his pulpit work, in his Sunday School administration, in the "training" of his class leaders, in the "normal" lines of his Sunday School supervision and direction, and in "special classes" devoted to the study of "pedagogy" as adapted to home and Sunday School instruction. He should be a special enthusiast and student in the department of education as carried on in the public school. He should be a subscriber to the strongest and best periodical of the country devoted to the subject of secular education. His pulpit work would be vastly benefited by this. His Sunday School would soon begin to show the results of this interest. The advantage of such intelligent instruction by the pastor would to no slight degree benefit the public school teachers and pupils connected with his Church and congregation. And as a result (not likely at first to be appreciated by himself or his people) the religious value of "day school" and of Sunday School work would be greatly increased in the circle of

1. *Northwestern Christian Advocate*, Vol. 58, No. 35, pages 20 and 31.

his personal and official influence. The work of a pastor includes a great deal more than the preaching of two sermons a Sunday, an occasional "talk" to his Sunday School, and a "season" of "special effort" with or without the assistance of a "revivalist" sometime during the winter. "Occasionalism" in Church life is a bane rather than a blessing. Special meetings derive their real value from the everyday insistent and persistent policy and spirit of the man who trains his people to believe in the ever-present, the ever-eager, the ever-ready divine spirit of "grace and truth," whose gospel he proclaims from the beginning to the end of every year of his pulpit and pastoral service.

There is such a wide and varied field opened to the pastor and preacher! Early in my ministerial life I resolved as a pastor to care for all departments of Church work. The statements I now make are not made in any spirit of boasting. God knows I have no justification for even the mildest form of self-exaltation, for either the secret or the public, the personal or official life I am now trying to report. What I may not tell to men I have often talked about to the gracious God, and with him left all the records and from him accepted whatsoever he may ordain in time and in eternity. And there is so much in this hidden and divine record of which I am heartily ashamed that what I do write concerning myself, my work, and my methods has really no shadow of egotism in it.

In my pastorate I tried to reach and affect for good every department of the work committed to me. I took a special interest in the children and youth. I kept a record of all the children connected in any way with the families of my congregation. This list I carried in my pocket most of the time, indicating by a mark those who had been baptized, those "on probation," those in "full membership," greeted them, became acquainted with them, talked at every opportunity with them, made them feel that they were a part of my "flock." I held the Saturday afternoon "Palestine class" which most of those old enough to know what it meant regularly attended. I held a "probationers' class." I urged the attendance of all children connected with the families of my Church upon the public service. I distributed literature adapted to them. I ran the risk of being called (a matter I much deprecated) "the children's preacher." I sought through a "normal class" and the "teachers' meeting" to encourage among all teachers and parents the study of the best methods of teaching little children.

Thus, I honestly endeavored to secure that even balance of administrative policy that permitted no side of pastoral responsibility to be overlooked. While I may never have even approximated my ideal of the pastor's obligation, I did constantly feel that every member of every family in my flock formed a part of the burden that rested upon me as one of the great Teacher's under shepherds.

Concerning the Christian ministry, I have always been an enthusiast. To me it is the most honorable, and certainly the most beautiful, of all "callings." I was, in a sense, born into it. By my precious mother I was consecrated to it from my earliest years. I really entered upon its duties prematurely – before I was eighteen years of age. My election long afterward to the episcopacy was a great surprise. When the suggestion was first made to me it seemed an impossibility. It became a reality. I think I can truthfully say that when the fact of my election to the episcopacy was announced, the gratification which I felt was not from the "honor" of it, nor the increase of official power it brought, nor yet the opportunity for wider travel. But I think it was in this: The office was sure to give me greater opportunity and authority in setting forth, especially to young ministers, the rare privilege (which, by the way, so few young preachers seem to appreciate), of holding up before the preachers and pastors of American Methodism the splendid opportunities in our day and under our civilization – not merely of being leaders in a great Church, and preachers of a gospel that offers eternal life to the sons of men, but of being pastors who have access to homes, to fathers and mothers, and to whom these ministers may, if they will, come with the high commission to bring up a generation of youths who shall become the fathers and mothers for a favored generation representing within the next century the highest type of culture, society, and religion that the race has even known. This side of the eternal heavens are rising generations of men and women who are to constitute a "this world" civilization – and the people whom we as ministers now hold in our hands for culture and Christianization are the "to be" fathers and mothers of that golden future. Wise indeed is that pastor who devotes himself to the noble task of raising up in his Church such homes, such fathers, such mothers.

It follows that the chief duty of the ministry and the Church is not to put forth occasional and special and sometimes somewhat frantic endeavors to "save souls" from the "everlasting fires." It is rather their mission to build up a strong, earnest, sane and effective present civilization, including home, school, sanctuary, ballot box, state house, daily and weekly press, and public library that our whole civilization may become sacred, all legitimate lines of occupation having printed boldly on them, "Holiness unto the Lord."

This is the emphasis which by the wise providence of God and the study of the strongest literature of these modern days it has become my highest ambition to set forth. It would be impossible for me to tell the story of my life were I to omit this radical emphasis which a certain class of the best modern literature has boldly and attractively and most effectively presented to the thoughtful minds of the present age. And I should certainly fail to do justice to those who have most helped me were I not to pay tribute to such men as Bushnell, William Arthur, Robertson of Brighton, Bowne of Boston University, and Robert Browning – but why attempt the calling of the roll of royal souls who as seers have spoken and sung words of awakening and enlarging and upbuilding in the age in which we live?

The work of the pastorate embraces not merely the proclamation of the gospel and the exposition of Scripture and Sunday sermons, and week evening Bible classes, the teaching of the catechism to little children, and the guiding of young people into paths of safety, the visiting of the poor and the afflicted, and the burying of the dead. The pastor has more than that to do. He is a leader in all the things that make for the strength and beauty of life. Wherever the people to whom he preaches and over whom he exercises pastoral supervision are required to go, he too should go, or have gone, that he might know the way they travel – the perils of it and the opportunities of it. Whatever in business, study, recreation, observation, and experience may give his people broader horizons, expose them to peculiar perils, open their eyes to new relations and impose other responsibilities – there the pastor should be able to go that he may the more thoroughly understand the difficulties they encounter and the demands duty makes upon them.

In the light these wide and varied relations sustained by the preacher and pastor it will be clearly seen that the man who undertakes the work of pulpit and pastorate has more to do than to pray in private and to preach in public. He must be a "man of the world." He must "know men." He must know the manners of the refined world and the sane and everyday views of the so-called "common place" people. His must be the standpoint that it may be the viewpoint of the average man of the world and of the Church to which he preaches. It is for this reason that so many men succeed in the ministry who have not been "highly" or "liberally" educated, and that so many fail in spite of the most thorough collegiate and professional training. He who has sense, common sense, a knowledge of human nature, familiarity with the Book of books, an unselfish devotion to humanity, an experience of the "things of the Spirit," who is interested in human society and is full of the philanthropic spirit and who gives himself to the study of man, society, the great political and reformatory movements of the world – is bound, sooner or later, to become a "scholar" and an able and successful preacher of the truth as it is in Christ, and all this whether he be a "college" and "seminary" graduate or not. Of one thing we may always be assured – that he will always be humble, self-forgetful, zealous, and successful in whatever field of labor he tries to do the will of God and advance the well-being of the race.

CHAPTER 24

# The Autobiography of Bishop Vincent

# Twenty-first Paper[1]

***September 21, 1910***

My assignment to Europe as resident bishop for the quadrennium 1901-04 was both a surprise and a source of pleasure. I had visited the Continent – the first time in 1862-63 and several times after that. On that first visit I had gone to the East, visiting Egypt, Palestine, Asia Minor, Greece, and Constantinople. On another trip, accompanied by my wife and son, I covered the same ground. I was in a sense familiar with the Continent and knew something of the religious conditions, especially in Germany and Switzerland. I was glad to be assigned to that field of service.

There are those among us, and among them many Methodists, who ask in all seriousness why we should be in Europe at all, as representatives of a denomination of Protestants. Are there not Protestants everywhere in Europe? Why, therefore, should we as Methodists, especially as American Methodists, be in Italy, Germany, Scandinavia, Switzerland, and Finland?

Of course, we are in Europe by invitation. Not that the Pope of Rome or the clergy of any of the Protestant Churches of the

1. *Northwestern Christian Advocate*, Vol. 58, No. 38, pages 12-13.

Continent invited us. Methodism as a providential movement in the modern world has not waited to be "called" by the state or free Churches of any country. The vital truths which Methodism has from the beginning of the great English Reformation under the Wesleys constantly and vigorously emphasized made inevitable a distinct ecclesiastical movement. The awakening of the nations to the reality of a vital, personal, subjective spiritual life compelled an organization and aggressive methods which were fresh, earnest, practical, and especially adapted to the demands of the times and of the new message and policy which the "fathers" were providentially compelled to introduce. And one of the most interesting features of this development is the close resemblance between this latest expression of genuine evangelicalism and the phenomena which are recorded in the New Testament as characterizing the initiation of the gospel in the beginning. Intensity in personal conviction, the burden of sin, the longing for deliverance, the bold, plain, simple, glad proclamation of pardon and peace and the witness of the Spirit by men and women who had themselves experienced the reality of it all, and the immediate transformation of individuals, families, and communities – all these things were as real as in the first century of the Christian dispensation. And there were enough testimonies on record from earlier ages, and from the later centuries, in the biographies of devout souls through all the centuries to make this Wesleyan revival simply a demonstration of what the gospel of Christ was given to the world to accomplish in the souls of men.

Now Methodism in America (where there were no state Church restrictions and where the people were free from old country prejudices) at once developed into a great revival and aggressive agency. Methodism grew and became strong. City and country, Northland and Southland, welcomed the new message.

Revival followed revival. Thousands of people, rich and poor, natives and foreigners, white and black, were "converted" and became bold witnesses for Christ. Wisdom did not always and everywhere prevail, but out of noise and oratory and house-to-house visitation and personal appeal and a simple, fervent, persistent effort, public and private, by the use of the living voice and the demonstration of earnest living on the part of thousands who had up to this time been worldlings and even worse – the cause of Christ prevailed. All denominations were built up, immorality received rebuke, Sabbath days were honored, and even the skeptical scholars and the more refined representatives of the "best society" confessed that the hand of God was in the movement.

Out of this great awakening for which Methodism was in part responsible, and the distinctive features of which Methodism always emphasized, our Church stood forth before the great American people as the ecclesiastical representative of vital Christianity, a clear inward witness of the blessedness of the spiritual life and an aggressive evangelistic and spiritual agency for the development of a thoroughly Christian civilization. Any minister or Church member in any denomination who boldly stood up for Christ and a vital experience was called "a Methodist."

Now it was this emphasis of Methodism – the earnest, positive inner life, "the joy of salvation" – that reached sincere immigrants from Germany, Scandinavia, Switzerland, and elsewhere. And it was here in the United States many of them for the first time learned that there was a piety of this type possible to any and all believers, rich and poor, cultivated and ignorant; and in "revival" meetings or under earnest sermons even where no revival was in progress, scores and hundreds of these people from across the Atlantic entered into this new, positive, and joyful life. Of course, the good news was told in letters and there were men ready to go back to their old land and as evangelists proclaim this vital type of the gospel. Preachers were sent to Germany, Switzerland, and elsewhere. The seed sown in quiet corners yielded a harvest. A call was made for more ministers of the new faith. Small societies were organized, "class meetings" were held, conferences were soon organized. And what with the Wesleyans from England and the awakening of evangelical zeal in all the Churches through other than Methodist agencies the earnest life of a vital Christianity was promoted in Europe and we now have Methodist Episcopal annual conferences in Germany, Italy, Bulgaria, Norway, Sweden, Denmark, Switzerland, Finland, and a new mission in France. We cooperate with evangelical believers in all the Churches of Europe. Our ministers are respected, and many are the earnest souls in all the Church there who seek the Methodist minister in times of special spiritual need. And while there are millions of people on the continent who attend no Church at all there is every reason why we as Methodists should do all we can to tell the story of Bethlehem, Calvary, and Olivet to the prodigal, the outcast, the neglected, and the Pharisee in the cities, on the plains, and among the mountains of Europe.

It is not only the vital emphasis we make as a Church in Europe but we take with us the spirit of democracy, of fraternity, and of equality which appeals to the people of Europe to-day possibly more than ever. We represent American ideas. We are from a country where so many of the people now have relatives and they become interested in us and our message because we come from the great land to which "brother," "son," "neighbor," "daughter," "friends" have gone.

Again, we have a great advantage in the peculiar type of "Christian union" which has developed in America in which denominational emphasis and Christian cooperation and sympathy are so complete as to promote real catholicity and at the same time appeal to a larger number and a greater variety of people. We are *one* and yet as "denominations" differ in government, order of service, and creed emphasis. Thus, a larger number of people may have what they prefer in the statement of doctrine and in the type of public service – extemporaneous, liturgical, or the two blended.

The activity of the Roman Church in filling this country with European representatives of a certain type, with an eye to gain one of these days at the polls, makes it necessary for us to do all that we can in the preparation of the Roman Catholic immigrant for a just appreciation of the true American civilization which is the very reverse of that in which as a loyal Romanist he has been trained on the other side. Every Roman Catholic should have every right that any native-born Protestant citizen can have under our flag, but we cannot teach the newcomer too emphatically his personal freedom from all ecclesiastical control as an American citizen. His first allegiance is to the nation.

My four years of official service in Europe were full of opportunity. The most cordial welcome was given me in conferences, parsonages, and in the clean, comfortable, and hospitable homes of our people. One need not master seven or more languages in order to administer as a bishop in Europe. I spoke English always. I soon learned to understand what the brethren were saying in their conference speeches and a good interpreter at my right hand made every obscure point clear as sunlight. And I did love to preach and talk through an interpreter. It made me condense what I had to say. It gave me a chance to think what I must "say next." It was pleasant to watch the faces of the brethren as they looked at me as I spoke as good English as I could and then they turned to the interpreter to make sure of what "the bishop was talking about."

O, a glorious set of men are those European Methodist preachers of ours! Straightforward, sincere, simple-hearted, consecrated to the Lord, devoted to the Church, loyal to their bishop whoever he may be, attentive to the work of training the children in the distinctive doctrines and usages of the Church, and as a rule blessed with a genuine Christian experience. I love them. I shall always be grateful to the Lord for the opportunity I enjoyed of spending four years in dear old Zurich and in being permitted to know and to love and to serve the Methodist preachers of our European Methodist Episcopal conferences.

CHAPTER 25

# The Autobiography of Bishop Vincent

## Twenty-second Paper[1]

***September 28, 1910***

When I was a boy I dreamed and dreamed of a journey to Europe, and when I became a man and a minister I extended my dream to embrace Egypt, Palestine, Asia Minor, and Greece. As a boy, clerking in my father's dry-goods store, I used to "play" travel, imagining myself on a foreign tour, and from day to day, without changing my habitat, going from place to place in Europe, extending my pilgrimage to the Holy Land and Egypt. There was but the slightest possibility that I should ever realize my dream. But I did.

I have made nine trips to Europe, two to Egypt and the Holy Land, and one to South America, crossing that continent from Buenos Aires to Santiago, going northward to, and crossing, the Isthmus of Panama on my return journey. I sailed up the Pacific as far as the Columbia River, and have crossed the North American continent several times.

I have always loved to travel, am fond of change, and on my official journeys have carried on (thanks to Pullman possibilities) business, studies, correspondence just as I should have done in my

1. *Northwestern Christian Advocate,* Vol. 58, No. 39, pages 11-12.

library at home. I love to be "on the go." It stimulates me to think, to write, to invent. Indeed, the Pullman at full speed, with a section to myself, table, books, and documents at hand, stimulates me to the best kind of work I am able to accomplish. I long ago learned to adjust myself to the motion of the car on the roughest railway, and take pleasure in proving how smoothly I can write even on a common day-car, at from twenty-five to fifty miles an hour. I have never met a serious accident and with one exception have never had an extremely uncomfortable time at sea.

That one exceptional experience is worth reporting, although I find a deal more pleasure in telling about than in experiencing it. We had left the island of Malta *en route* for Egypt. We encountered at the start a terrible storm. The wind was violent and from the east, and when a few – perhaps thirty – miles east of the island during the night I woke up to feel the ship rolling from side to side and not resisting the great waves as she had been doing ever since we left the port of Valletta. Calling a waiter, I asked what was the matter. He replied, "Matter enough. We have lost our rudder, are rolling in the trough of the sea, and are drifting toward the eastern coast of Malta." That startled and alarmed me. I at once realized our peril. Unless the rudder could be controlled, we were doomed to drift until we were wrecked on the reefs of Malta. But there was nothing to do but to lie still as the rolling ship would allow and wait for what might happen.

There was no comfort in thinking of "an experience to tell." Nor could I gather for myself any consolation from the fact that "this is the very place and situation St. Paul was once in." I felt too little like St. Paul in personal character or in the immediate object of my mission to derive any consolation from the fact that "once Paul was here." The reflection did not at all appeal to me; nor did it quiet my fears. I confess that in the alarm of the hour I did not find comfort in prayer, although I think I did pray. I was nervous and restless and uncomfortable. And how glad I was when some hours later I felt the rolling ship respond to the pressure of the rudder. I knew then that it was all right. And with a word of thanksgiving, I turned over and committed myself to the embrace of sleep. And when a few hours later I awoke the stateroom was radiant with morning sunlight and the steady movement of the ship assured me that we were on a quiet sea.

How glad and grateful I was! And then I prayed for a more positive and steady faith in the guiding hand of a gracious God. And I was and since then have always been humiliated by the remembrance of my feeble faith where Paul's was so strong, and where mine should have been equally strong. But that was not the only experience of my poor life in which the contrast was so sharply drawn between the courageous apostle and the timid pilgrim from the Far West. And really the "pleasure in telling" to which I referred in the beginning of this narration is very slight. It makes one pray for more courage and for a clearer, keener, and more comfortable faith in the presence and in the providential care of our Father in Heaven. What a contrast we often find between the "consolations" and the "supporting power of faith" as we talk about them in pulpit and prayer meeting and as we experience them in the actual struggles and exigencies of everyday life! O, Lord: Increase our faith!

I shall not here enter into the details of my trip through Northern Egypt nor the story of my journey through Palestine in 1863. There was quite a company of us – chiefly ministers of four or five different denominations who met in Jerusalem and after an interesting visit to Bethlehem, Hebron, the Jordan, and the Dead Sea started one golden morning for the North. We traveled on horseback – there were fifteen or twenty of us.

The Sunday we were in Jerusalem I was invited to preach on the summit of the Mount of Olives, and about ten o'clock we crossed the valley of Kidron, passed the Garden of Gethsemane, and climbed the rugged heights of the mountain, and, finding a place overlooking the city and the temple area – the Moriah of Scripture – we sang a hymn, a prayer was offered by one of the American preachers then visiting the city, and I preached from the words: "And they came to the Mount of Olives." It was a beautiful and impressive opportunity. The occasion and the place were in themselves a sermon. Human words were almost out of place. Mountain and valley and garden, the silent and venerable city stretching out below and beyond us, the temple area where once Jesus stood – all these were a silent and an eloquent sermon.

The advantage of such an opportunity is rather sentimental than real. It is transitory. Indeed, the mind may be so occupied with the sentiment suggested by the locality as to lose all its spiritual and ethical value. Looking at "the things that are seen" may easily divert the soul's attention from the things unseen, real and eternal. The effect of life in the land of Palestine, the city of Jerusalem, the town of Nazareth, or even by the shore of the Sea of Galilee is not really conducive to the spiritual life. "Not on this mountain," said Jesus. And he said the immortal words, "God is a spirit," and he is to be worshiped "in spirit and in truth."[1] Where man is most in need of divine help, there God is. "Where two or three are gathered together in the name" of Jesus Christ, there Christ is, and there is ready to do for man what he has promised, as man conforms to the conditions prescribed.[2] Christ is as near to the devout miner in the dark depths of the mountain as he

1. John 4:21-24.
2. Matthew 18:20.

was to his disciples on the summit of Olivet or in the Garden of Gethsemane.

Life abroad is interesting and valuable not only because of the suggestions one receives concerning the long past and the events and personal characters of which one is reminded, but one has opportunity now and then to come in contact with men of national reputation, and now and then with men whose fame and influence are literally world-wide. On my first visit to London in 1862 I had the pleasure of hearing Mr. Spurgeon in his famous Tabernacle.[3] I listened to one of his earnest, practical, and really inspiring sermons, and after the service slipped into his private study and had a pleasant interview with him. In the course of our conversation, I asked him when he expected to visit America. He replied promptly and with a smile, "After the day of judgment." I congratulated him on his just estimate of the character and blessedness of my native land.

I had the good fortune on one of my visits to London to be invited to a luncheon at the city residence of Dr. Joseph Parker, the famous Congregational preacher. He had invited Mr. Gladstone to be his guest that the great statesman might have opportunity to present to a company of the "dissenting ministers" of London some reasons for the political position which he had been compelled to take.[4]

There were probably twenty ministers present. The lunch was simple but ample, and few were present who cared for anything except the opportunity of seeing at close range and of hearing the

3. Charles Spurgeon (1834-1892) served as pastor of Metropolitan Tabernacle, London, for 38 years.

4. William E. Gladstone served as Prime Minister of the United Kingdom 1868-1874, 1880-1885, February to July 1886, and 1892-1894.

words of Mr. Gladstone. I accounted it a great privilege (one of the greatest of my life) to sit for more than an hour – two hours in fact – very near to the distinguished English statesman and to hear him make his earnest appeal designed to conciliate and to secure the sympathy of the "dissenting ministers" of the country. Gladstone had an impressive presence, was frank, earnest, and cordial; made a clear and forcible exposition of the measure he was seeking to carry through. He stated his case, skillfully elicited the opinions of the gentlemen whom he was anxious to win to the side of the government; and whatever may have been the final conviction of the company on the question then pending, I am sure that all were delighted to have been permitted to sit for two hours in the close and instructive fellowship of this greatest of modern British statesmen.

While abroad for any length of time a thoughtful American gets into the way of looking at his country and his fellow countrymen from a new point of observation. And one cannot forget the adverse criticisms which he has read or heard from both European and American travelers concerning his fellow countrymen. When an American so far forgets the dictates of loyalty as to even speak lightly of his fellow countrymen in the presence of foreigners, however just the criticism may be, he needs a lesson in loyalty and courtesy. One may be ready to smile at the infirmities of the American when he is canvassing the subject with Americans, but when an Englishman or other representative of the Eastern Hemisphere attempts to disparage the American "kind" it is to him as though an assault had been made upon his own kin.

There are some uncomfortable peculiarities which betray themselves in Americans of a certain type abroad, and it is embarrassing to a refined and sensitive American to detect them, but he should be too much of an American gentleman to hold up to ridicule, especially in the presence of a foreigner, one who belongs to his own national household. There are weak men – and women – who travel abroad. But they may not always be deserving of ridicule and contempt. Sensitive, self-conscious, timid, easily embarrassed, really anxious for the sake of his country to make a good impression on the strangers he meets, one may entirely misrepresent himself. Such misfortune is ground for sympathy and furnishes self-possessed people an opportunity for the noblest type of ingenuity in smoothing the way for people less favored. It is a great thing to be a gentleman, refined, self-forgetful, and so absorbed with the aim to make other people comfortable that he not only never causes, but naturally, spontaneously overcomes embarrassment in others.

As a rule, the American in England is treated with great respect. I was in England in 1862 when the "war" was on, and the best English people were divided into two classes: Those who sympathized with the North and those who, while they did not favor slavery, were quite willing that the republic should be weakened by division and the demonstration made to the whole world that the republican form of government was impracticable – anywhere and everywhere. The failure of secession and the destruction of slavery changed the feeling of all classes in Europe, and now it is an honor everywhere beyond the Atlantic to be introduced as "an American."

CHAPTER 26

# The Autobiography of Bishop Vincent

## Twenty-third Paper[1]

***October 5, 1910***

Once or twice I have referred to the "Palestine Class" for a Saturday afternoon study of sacred history and geography. As pastor I held a Palestine class on Saturday afternoons during my pastorates in Irvington, N. J., Joliet, Mount Morris, Galena and Rockford, Ill. – from 1855 to 1865. It was the object of this class to emphasize the geographical and historical contents of the Bible, and to do it in a way that must prove pleasant and exciting to the young folks who must have Saturday pleasure and it must be attractive and interesting enough to overcome the passion for romp and play for which well-brought-up children come to think that Saturday afternoon was really made.

Having made the experiment in Irvington, N. J., for nearly or quite two years, when I was appointed to Joliet in 1857 I resolved to make the experiment with my Western congregation. An invitation was extended to old and young of all denominations and on Saturday afternoon, May 23, 1857, the first meeting was held in the old Joliet Church lecture room.

1. *Northwestern Christian Advocate*, Vol. 58, No. 40, pages 12-13.

On my desk and now open before me as I write, is the old "Record Book" of all my Palestine classes and the names of the members – from 1855 to1864. Here are the grades, "Pilgrims," "Residents," "Explorers," "Dwellers in Jerusalem," and here the "Templars." The minutes of the several classes are in large part in this old record book. While in Mount Morris we wrote a series of letters and published them in the local paper, the class taking an imaginary tour through the Bible world, and reporting to the home paper from week to week. This gave a realistic touch to our weekly "play study." The "exhibitions" were public illustrations of the work the class was carrying on. Dialogues, chants, songs, addresses, simultaneous recitations, map tests – and thus the historical, geographical, and archeological portions of Scripture, with special emphasis on the biographical, developed an interest which prepared the way for the most direct ethical, doctrinal, and spiritual teachings. The Sunday sermons found response in the familiarity of so large a portion of the congregation with the externals, as they may be called, of the divine revelation.

The mastery in the realm of modern pedagogy might adversely criticize the use of the simultaneous method for insuring innumerable repetitions of difficult biblical names; but the enthusiasm excited in the old Palestine classes by this concert method, and the thoroughness guaranteed by the most rigid personal examinations justified me at the time in the stress I placed on the attractive simultaneous and "play" features of our Saturday afternoon studies in Bible history and geography.

I am tempted to insert, if the Editor does not forbid, the "Chant of the Bible Lands," by which, with the aid of an outline map on which not a name appeared, every pupil, old and young, became perfectly familiar with the location of every country named in the Bible, as far as modern scholarship attempts to locate it. However ridiculous this may be made to appear as either a sarcastic or a jolly skeptic of the method may "rend" or render it, the memory of a class of two hundred, more or less, of old and young repeating this list as the long pointer of the leader passed from country to country, and later on, the individual examination in which the knowledge of each pupil was fairly tested – that experience not only justifies the method but brings sweet memories of an enthusiasm in the study of the Bible which I have never in my long life seen excelled.

The study of the "Holy Scriptures" in our day is the surest remedy for whatever harm may come from what is called "the higher criticism." Let us "search the Scriptures" as we have them. Let us emphasize the biography, the archaeology, the ethics, the unfolding of the divine character as revealed in Jesus Christ, the subjective spiritual life as everywhere urged upon us, and all the doubts that can be started concerning the "letter" or the "human element in revelation" will vanish as does the hoar frost of the morning when the sun rises. What we need is not skill in the modern art of criticism (against which I have not one word to say here) but a knowledge of the Christ as he is set forth in these holy pages, and the knowledge of him as a present Saviour from the sin of the heart and from the sins of the age will so fill us with divine enthusiasm that we shall have no fear from the scorn of the scoffer, the challenge of the skeptic, or the apathy of the neglectful and obdurate worlding. More study of Bible history, Bible geography, Bible archeology, Bible biography, Bible ethics, Bible doctrines and Bible experience, and the unity and the divinity of the Book as a whole will appear and the reverent higher critics will be found to have contributed to an intelligent faith in and loyalty to the great Book of books – THE HOLY BIBLE.

Another department of Church work to which I have given especial attention is the Sunday School. It was long a matter of regret that I should be called "a Sunday School man." I was interested in Sunday School from my childhood. In my very early ministry I "looked after" the Sunday Schools of my circuit and stations. But I have from the beginning placed the Sunday School in subordination to the pulpit, or rather have sought to recognize both as divinely originated – the first to proclaim the gospel, to defend it, and to persuade men to become "disciples," and the second to edify, establish, and strengthen the disciples. The best kind of a Sunday School is a Church class meeting – not a certain type of class meeting that is always feeling after "feeling," and talking in unnatural tones under a sort of "holy" embarrassment, calling it "giving testimony to personal experience," and all that. By a class meeting I mean a simple, natural, earnest, "conversation" about the work of grace needed in our houses, shops, fields, voting booths, in our recreations, and in the training of our own children to play, to pray, to vote, to transact business in a divine way – and whatever else makes for a really Christian civilization. And we need to remember that all social reform must depend upon the personal, vital, spiritual experience of the individual.

The emphasis I have tried to make as preacher and pastor and as bishop is the emphasis on a type of personal life insisted upon by Drummond, by Bushnell, by Professor Bowne, by Robertson, by William Arthur in his "Tongue of Fire," by Professor Horne of Dartmouth in the "Psychological Principles of Education." If I had my way I should have every young preacher of the Church to-day (and the older preachers who forget that they are over twenty) take a course of special study in religious psychology, with the understanding that the course is not taken as intellectual stimulus but as a means of grace and of renewed personal surrender to God that they might know what Paul meant when he wrote that part of his letter to the Ephesians recorded in chapter 3:14-21. The greatest need of the ministry today is the positive *experience* of the gospel we are to-day commissioned to preach. Is this "commonplace"? Would God that it were more "common." Would God that in my earlier years I had appreciated it more. Then in my later years I should have been saved from many sources of bitter regret.

What better use can I make of my own experience than as an old man to offer these words of advice to the young men of today who are now entering upon the noble work of Christian ministry. Let me do it then in the closing words of the chapter. It holds the secret of the Christian's success.

Seek, and if you seek honestly, you are sure to have – an "understanding with God" every day. Therefore, take time for daily converse with God. Talk to him a great deal. Don't always say, "thou." Sometimes say "you" when you talk to God. The "thou" sometimes puts a barrier between you and the loving, sympathetic, near-at-hand, gentle Friend and Father. He is more motherlike than we realize. A dear, reverent, trusting, loving soul now and then in his private prayer said, "O God, my Mother and Father, hear my prayer." And when you pray, don't always feel that you must "kneel down." You "live and move and have your being in God" – therefore "pray without ceasing," at any time, in any place, in any posture, in the midst of any activity. Pray while you walk, wash dishes, "put the room to rights," dig in the garden, shovel snow from the sidewalk – "pray without ceasing." After a while and before very long you will pray in all you do. Let prayer become your way of breathing in the realm of spirit. Feel free to ask God for anything. The getting the thing you ask for is not the principal thing in prayer. There is a good deal to be had by prayer beside this. There is something in sunlight even though your eyes be closed. One breath of petition born of a holy desire to be in fellowship with God, accompanied by a resolve, even while sweeping the room or arranging the library for a day's work, may open a celestial door that will let in a breath of heaven into your life and fill your day with holy rapture.

Thus, I have closed this chapter as all the old Methodist preachers did every sermon – "with a benediction."

CHAPTER 27

# The Autobiography of Bishop Vincent

## Twenty-fourth Paper[1]

***October 26, 1910***

In my episcopal administration I sought to continue my work as both preacher and teacher, to which mission I was ordained in the beginning of my official career. At all the conferences where I presided, I used the opening devotional services every day as opportunity for emphasis upon the use of the Word of God. From my first conference I always conducted a morning service of Bible study and prayer, taking Paul's letters to Timothy as the foundation of all that as bishop I had to say, especially, to the young men of the conference, illustrating in connection with ministries of praise and prayer the possibility of Scripture exposition as an aid to devotion. What Paul wrote in the first century to his beloved Timothy, the young men as ministers of the Word need to-day. These devotional hours of the conference were usually crowded with preachers, laymen, earnest women and citizens of the town, and afforded the bishop opportunity to say many things helpful to the laity and to the community at large as well as to the ministry. When I presided over an annual

1. *Northwestern Christian Advocate*, Vol. 58, No. 43, pages 10-11.

conference a second time, I made use of Paul's letters to the Ephesians in the same manner.

Another feature which I introduced into my conduct of most of my annual conferences was the employment of some scholarly and earnest representative of the "larger thought" of the Christian faith who every morning enriched the "devotional hour" preceding the business session of the conference by a series of lectures especially adapted to the ministry and interesting also to the community at large.

My plan was based upon my own experience and observations as a young man in the ministry. A bishop comes to an annual conference with large authority given to him by the Church, and the average Methodist preacher, with his reverence for the Church and the General Conference, receives the bishop as having authority and as being qualified to give advice especially to the young men of the annual conference. However mistaken this judgment may be, the bishop himself has ample justification for assuming the attitude of instructor and inspirer, especially to the young men in the ministry. It is possible to make the morning devotional service of an annual conference a formal function – to appoint venerable and devout men to conduct it. But here is where the bishop's ministry in the department of spiritual life exerts its largest and greatest influence. It may demand more service from him than he feels able to render. At the same time, it is a peculiar opportunity for the emphasis among his brethren in the ministry of the spiritual life of which he and they are representatives in every community.

The letters of Paul to Timothy are remarkable documents. The opportunity for exposition and application by the bishop in his use of these letters has a value that can scarcely be overestimated. The more one studies the letters of Paul to Timothy the more profoundly he is impressed with the practical wisdom, the spiritual insight, and the teaching skill of the great apostle. The most able men, the most skillful and practical thinkers of modern times, could not have presented the principles underlying the ethical, social, and spiritual problems of this age more fully than does Paul in his letters to Timothy. I account it a rare opportunity that a bishop has for emphasizing the teachings of Paul to both the laity and the ministry as they are presented in these remarkable epistles.

Another advantage of this devotional ministry at the annual conference is the emphasis which the bishop himself is able to make on expository preaching. Not that he or any other preacher may be a master of the art of exposition, but the emphasis which Paul makes in these letters and the practical application of Christian doctrine as adapted to every community in our own times must have its effect upon every preacher and every layman who listens to this episcopal deliverance. We need in our ministry more biblical exposition. Where ministers expound the Scriptures from week to week, bringing out the value of prophetic, ethical, doctrinal, and subjective instruction there conveyed, he will need, and the people will need, very little of the apologetic element in the pulpit. The Scriptures carry with them their own defense, and I should like to emphasize this single thought – the value of expository preaching for the really most effective pastoral service.

All men do not have the gift, but "practice makes perfect," and our age needs a new emphasis upon the intrinsic value of the Book of books and the wonderful adaptation of its contents to the age of advanced and progressive thought in which we live. It was this conviction that led me to use that golden hour at the opening of every annual conference session in the exposition of Scripture, especially as that Scripture sets forth ministerial and ecclesiastical principles and responsibilities.

Another department of Church work to which I have given especial attention is the Sunday School. I regretted for years that I was known as "a Sunday School man." I have always feared "hobbies" and the "hobbyists." I was always interested in Sunday School work as was my father before me. But from the beginning I placed this department of church activity in subordination to the pulpit, or, rather, have sought to seek the recognition of both as of divine origin and having equal divine authority. But first, for the minister – *The Pulpit*, the mission of which is to proclaim the gospel, to define and to defend it, and to persuade men to become "disciples;" and then of necessity must come *The School* to enlighten, edify, establish, and strengthen the disciples won by the pulpit.

The best kind of Sunday or Church School is the class meeting – not, indeed, a certain type of class meeting that is always feeling after "feeling" and talking in unnatural tones, under a sort of "holy" embarrassment, calling it "giving testimony" to personal experience and all that. By the class meeting I mean a simple, natural, earnest "conversation" about the work of grace needed and sought, for the increased effectiveness of our homes, shops, fields, voting booths, recreations, and in the training of our own children to play, to pray, to study, to transact business in a divine way – and to advance whatever else makes for a really Christian civilization. And we need to remember that all permanent social and even genuine political reform must at the last depend upon the personal ideals and vital spiritual quality of the individual.

Therefore in all my life as a preacher, pastor, and bishop I have sought to put great emphasis on the type of personal faith and life – which has been in these later years insisted upon vigorously, brilliantly, and most wisely by Henry Drummond, William Arthur, Horace Bushnell, Robertson of Brighton, and lately by Professor Horne in his noble book on "Psychological Principles of Education."

If I could have my way I should have every young preacher of the Church (and the older preachers who forget that they are over twenty years of age) take a course of special study in religious psychology with the understanding that the course is not taken chiefly for intellectual stimulus but as a means of grace accompanied by a renewal of personal surrender to God that they night better understand what Paul meant when he wrote that part of the Epistle to the Ephesians recorded in chapter 3:14-21. The greatest need of the ministry to-day is the positive personal experience of the gospel we are this day commissioned to preach. It this "commonplace"? Would to God it were more "common" among us! Would to God that in my earlier years I had appreciated it more. Then in my later years I should have been saved from many sources of bitter regret. This emphasis is the imperative need of the Church to-day. It may not always contribute to the preacher's reputation as an "orator," nor as a man "who is up to the times," as the phrase goes nowadays, but it calls the attention of the people away from the *man* to the Word, from rhetoric to the truth that convinces, converts, and clothes with power the follower of Christ and his apostles. Expository preaching is not at "a premium," as we say nowadays, but it *is* "the power of God unto salvation." I have often wished that every young man in our ministry could have heard the distinguished Dr. John Hall of the Fifth-avenue Presbyterian Church in New York as he interpreted and applied the teaching of Christ, his apostles, and the prophets who foretold his mission to the world. It is the Word of God that awakens, startles, allures, converts, edifies, and establishes the simple "believer." It is this Word we are set to proclaim and apply. The more learning, scriptural and scientific, sacred and secular, the preacher has at command, the more effectually he may be able to arrest attention, awaken interest, kindle enthusiasm, and win to lifelong discipleship the people who come to the sanctuary where he is preacher and pastor.

In our early ministry as a Church the "fathers" gave attention to the reading and study of the Holy Scriptures. Plain men they were but strong men – established in the faith, the teachings of the Word in command, promise, and doctrine at their tongue's end. Dwight L. Moody of Chicago (and now of the whole world) was an admirable illustration of what many of the early Methodist preachers were – men of power, of profound experience in the things of the Spirit, of tremendous earnestness, with whole pages of the Holy Scriptures at command. How well I knew the dear Moody, when he was a Bible-class teacher and an aggressive evangelistic worker in Chicago! How in Dublin, in the elegant home the fervent layman whom we called "Father Bewley," with a company of earnest laymen from London and other parts of England, did our simple-hearted, consecrated Moody set forth the possibilities of the more earnest life and the methods of effective evangelism. Never shall I forget the week I was permitted to spend in that lovely home with those earnest Irishmen, Englishmen, and Scotchmen as it were at Moody's feet, now plying him with questions, now listening to his expositions of Scripture, now joining with him in fervent prayer for the "gift" of spiritual power.

May the gracious God give us in this day scores of such consecrated men in the ministry and in the laity!

(To be concluded.)

CHAPTER 28

# The Autobiography of Bishop Vincent

# Concluding Paper[2]

*November 2, 1910*

In the review of my episcopal work, as recorded in pocket notes in my calendars and in other personal and private records of the several annual conferences, at home and abroad, over which I presided during the brief period of my episcopal service – from 1888 to 1904 – I find that in these conferences at the early devotional hours and during the regular conference sessions and at occasional afternoon and evening services, as well as at sessions of what I called "The Itinerants' Club," held in different parts of the country, I was in the habit of discussing questions ecclesiastical, educational, doctrinal, and spiritual, aiming to interest the younger men (and the older men who did not know that they were not still young) in such topics as the following: "The Minister's Care of his Physical Health," "The Noble Possibilities of Country and Circuit Work," "Weekday Bible Teaching," "The Pastor's Interest in the Higher Education," "Out-of-school Culture," "The Art of Memory Training," "The Pastor and the Children and Youth of his Church," "The Possibilities of Adult Education," "The Preacher's Library," emphasizing the treasures to be found

2. *Northwestern Christian Advocate*, Vol. 58, No. 44, pages 12 and 27.

in Ruskin, Robertson, Bushnell, Bowne, Browning, and calling the attention of these preachers of to-morrow to the vast difference between "sensational and substantial Church work."

We need in our day to awaken in the laity a keen sense of responsibility for deeper sympathy of the home with the larger and more spiritual work of the Church. We are in danger of depending too much on "revivalism" and the professional evangelists and not enough on godly parents, daily family prayer, systematic and steady home religious endeavor in the training of every child under our care in the fundamentals of the Christian faith. The wisest evangelists of the age will tell you that their best work is accomplished when home, Sunday School, and pulpit are most faithful in setting forth the great evangelical doctrines, three hundred and sixty-five days every year.

Of course, this distinctive Christian work, steadily sustained, imposes a heavy burden upon the pastor and his official assistants. It means patient and unremitting labor twelve months every year. It means everyday faith. It means the evangelistic proclamation and appeal every week. It means personal endeavor year in and year out. In a Church making this emphasis, and persistent and consistent effort, sinners will turn to Christ and believers be built up in Christ at any season of the year, not waiting for Lenten or revivalistic times. And under this theory made practical, Lent will mean more and the Week of Prayer and the week of evangelistic effort, and every preaching service and every Sunday School session, all will mean more to preacher, believers, and penitents, because the whole Church gives her whole heart and her whole time to the one supreme mission of life: business, study, society, politics, worship – the whole of life surrendered in sane, steady, and unselfish service to the Eternal GOD and in the supreme

Christian endeavor to make sacred all things that belong to "the life that now is" in the interest of "the life that is to come."

No, this is not an impractical ideal. It is the standard set before us in the Holy Scriptures and in the life of Him who said, and now says, to every son of man: "FOLLOW THOU ME." When by the presence and sway of the Divine Spirit in the inmost soul one is able to say, "I will follow thee, O Lord, withersoever thou mayest lead me," then and then only shall man know the possibilities of a life in which the secular is made sacred. The "all things" of the divine promise embrace science, art, society, pleasure, Christian fellowship, philanthropic service, political activity, with the sweet and secret communion with God which the true believer has guaranteed to him. Then the planets, all of them, and the sun that holds them, shall be the glorious inheritance of him to whom the Father has said, "Thou art my child."

The whole of life having been thus appropriated by the believer, it is for him to enjoy and use the whole of life; to gain culture, so then the pastor's place and work become much more complicated which God has given him – one or two or ten; and to be content where his lot is cast, only so that he may make the world a better world, the race wiser, life nobler, and eternity more real. And this broad view of the Christian's calling and opportunity changes the view of life so common among a class of honest and earnest believers. If the theory here presented be the true one, then the pastor's place and work become much more complicated and difficult. He lives for what we may call the true Christian civilization, standing as it does for both time and eternity, forming a holy unity, all secular relations and responsibilities becoming sacred.

This, the twenty-fifth paper of the present series, may appropriately have to do with the closing of my experience and work as an "effective" bishop of the Church. The episcopal office in the

Methodist Episcopal branch of the Holy Catholic Church is an "office," and not an "order." The Church recognizes two orders in her ministry – deacons and presbyters (or elders). It is our theory that the *episcopoi* of the early Church were elders who, superintending certain interests of the Church, pastoral and general, received the title of bishops or superintendents.

The bishops with us are elected for life, that they may devote themselves wholly to this work of supervision. They are called "general superintendents." The bishops are relieved of all anxiety concerning their term of office, and therefore as long as they are able to serve the Church are accounted "effective," and on failure of health are placed on the "retired" list and continue as "bishops" to receive a comfortable support from the Church. They hold the office for life. A bishop may be apparently in impaired health for a time and unable for a brief period to fulfill his episcopal duties. He has rest and opportunity for recuperation, but when really disabled is placed on the "retired list." And the decision as to the matter of his effectiveness – that is made *for* him by those who are supposed to be better judges than he can possibly be, of his limitations and adaptation to the work of the episcopate. He is a wise man who accepts the situation with a reverent and cheerful "The will of the Lord and his Church be done." That surrender and acceptance are not always immediate and spontaneous but are sure to follow the suggestion of wisdom. It is the faith of our preachers and people that the grace and providence of God superintend the affairs of his Church. If bishops do not accept that theory, they need not wonder that the "appointments" they make in annual conference are sometimes challenged by their "appointees." Our Church theory of a divine providence in the ordering of Church governance and ministerial assignment is comfortable and wholesome as applied to bishops as when by bishops it is applied to "preachers in charge," whether they be men "on trial" or regularly accepted and ordained "members" of an annual conference.

In rereading the chapters of this autobiographic venture, I find, as no doubt my most generous readers have already remarked, "too much preaching." That is my infirmity. I began too early, and I have continued to exercise these gifts too long, and from my own domestic hearth (always noted for its candor) to the most generous group that has honestly tried (possibly in vain) to read these reminiscences, I can in my quiet study hear the same gentle but honest criticism – "too much moralizing, too much preaching."

Another personal word in closing this series of autobiographical chapters: During the years of my retirement from episcopal service I have been active in preaching, lecturing, writing, and holding many series of public services known as "Seven Days' Studies in Church Life." In these ministries, held in many parts of the country, I have met with gratifying success, speaking from three to six times every day, discussing questions relating to home, pulpit, day school, Sunday School, philanthropy, political responsibility from the Christian and Church point of view – and emphasizing the Christian's responsibility for self-culture, as illustrated by what is known as "the Chautauqua idea."

The Church of my childhood and of the choice of my manhood has been very good and generous to me from the day I was I inspired to prepare the first "lesson leaf" of the modern series of Sunday School lesson helps to the night when as an "effective" bishop I pronounced the benediction upon the last annual conference over which I was permitted to preside. I love with ardent affection our noble Church, a worthy branch of the Holy Catholic Church; and I give thanks to the good God who cares for the whole Church and, as dear Abraham Lincoln said, "who gives us all the Churches."

And now it is time for the benediction, which with too many little people, and with a goodly number of their seniors, comes to be accounted the most welcome and appropriate of all the functions of the public service. And to all my kind and patient readers I may express the hope that as the grace of the good God has already received into his own heavenly home the majority of the beloved ones whose lives have blessed and enriched my life, so may his grace long protect and long continue the earthly relationships of my readers, and in his own good time and in his own wise way bring us all into the blessed relations, reunions, recognitions, and raptures of the life celestial and eternal.

# Later Writings

1913-1915

CHAPTER 29

# John H. Vincent Letter to Rev. William Wood

***5700 Blackstone Ave.***
***CHICAGO***
***Dec. 18 '13***

Rev. William Wood
Kent's Hill, Me.

Dear Sir and Brother:

I do not like to write about myself, but you have asked, and it is proper for me as a brother to give you an answer. Therefore, on this leaf of paper that has "been in Jerusalem" I attempt to respond to your questions as briefly as I can.

I was brought up in a thoroughly Christian Home. My father (whose Father was of Huguenot descent but who became in his later life influenced by Unitarian associations and was 'liberal' in his religious views) was brought under Methodist influence in Tuscaloosa Alabama and there with my Mother (who had been baptized and confirmed in the Lutheran Church in Philadelphia) became a Methodist. I was therefore born, baptized, trained (and that strictly) in the intelligent, liberal, fervent and positive type of Methodism which is to be found in the South among the more cultivated people. The emphases of Presbyterian, Lutheran, Unitarian and Methodist doctrines and usages were thus in my blood, and made me positive in "orthodox" faith, liberal in judgment of all forms of faith and worship and "open" to light all the years of my childhood, youth and maturity. I have been intensely interested in the sermons, essays, lectures and writings of such men as Chalmers, Wesley, Robertson of Brighton, Maurice, Horace Bushnell, Drummond, and find inspiration in both Chalmers and – Swedenborg. I have learned the meaning of the statement "Good in all and none all-good". And the older I grow and the more I know of life the more real to me is the Master's statement "He that doeth my will shall know of the doctrine."[1]

Then I remember that as the world grows and as men develope [sic], and as the individual comes to care more for TRUTH than for "Institutions," and personally surrenders himself to philanthropic ministries and tries to make the world and its civilization better, he and those with whom he is most intimately associated are sure to come more closely together and to agree to disagree in interpretations, that experimentation on the individual and on society may be carried on scientifically and thoroughly, and the grandchildren of "day-after-tomorrow" in our civilization will be as loyal to TRUTH as we have desired them to be. I believe in "denominations" for this reson [sic] and while I love my own – the META ODOS – "after the Way" – people who follow Jesus who said, "I AM THE HODOS[2]" are sure if they do really follow HIM to come ultimately into "all truth".

I am afraid that in this self-indulgent mood I have failed to give you what you asked for.

I inherited from a saintly Mother a strong bias in favor of the religious life. She was of Lutheran origin but under the guidance,

1. From John 7:16-18.
2. From John 14:6, "I Am the way...."

teaching and companionship of earnest people in Tuscaloosa Ala. became a Methodist Episcopalian. She was a saint. My father, less saintly, was serious and conscientious and tried hard to be "good." And he was a worthy man who had to struggle against "circumstances" but who did bring up his children to honor God and to love the Church.

Now I don't know but that I have written too freely. I have not written for the press but for your own eyes and from this statement you can make a condensed paragraph.

Please let me have a line from you in response to this communication.

SINCERELY YOURS,

P.S. I never took a full college course. Was taught by a Home Governess; was a student in the Public School; in the Lewisburg (Pa) Academy; in the Preparatory department of the Lewisburg (Pa) University; in the Newark (N.J.) Wesleyan Institute; and then entered the Methodist Ministry taking the Four Years Course of Study required of all our Preachers. Then I took up a private Course of study covering the "College Student's Outlook" which afterwards led to my plan now known as "The Chautauqua Literary and Scientific Circle" which is a four years Course of Home Reading and Study which covers in English the old fashioned "College Curriculum." I have tried to turn the whole of life into a "course of study" and to encourage middle-aged and old people to think and to feel that it is never too late to read and think and grow and teach others to do the same.

## CHAPTER 30

# Bishop John H. Vincent at 83[3]

***February. 24, 1915***

Dear Brother Zaring:

You request a "birthday message" for February 23. On that date in 1832, my eyes saw the light in Tuscaloosa, Ala. When a child of six years (or about that time) our family moved to Pennsylvania, where on the banks of the Susquehannah [sic] River I lived until I entered the New Jersey Conference in 1853. In 1857 I was transferred to the Rock River Conference serving there in Joliet, Mount Morris, Galena, and Rockford, and Trinity in Chicago.

The emphasis I had made in my pastoral work on Sunday School organization, Bible study and the art of religious teaching led me into educational, editorial, and other pastoral ministries recognized and approved by the Church. As a pastor I held in nearly every "charge" to which I was assigned a Saturday afternoon class for the study of Bible biography, history, and geography. I began this in Irvington, N. J., in 1855. In 1857 I organized my second "Palestine Class" for Saturday afternoon Bible study in Joliet, Ill. This class plan for Saturday afternoon Bible work I kept up in Mount Morris, Galena, and Rockford, Ill. During these years I kept up private studies, under skillful direction, in Greek and Hebrew. Later I devised a plan for popular reading courses in the

3. *Northwestern Christian Advocate,* February 24, 1915, page 194.

fields of literature covered by the then popular college curriculum. By this method the field of college study in vogue in those days was made accessible for adults who not taking the regular linguistic course might become familiar with the world biographical, historical, literary and scientific embraced in the old-time college curriculum. This idea and plan are embodied in what is known as "The Chautauqua Literary and Scientific Circle." I go into details here because I firmly believe that the pastor should be the representative in his church and among his young people of the college world, and should do his best to send as many as possible of his young people to college. And I am sure that people of from thirty to eighty years should take up and keep up courses of reading in secular as well as in religious lines. It is a pity to see men or women of 80 or 85 indifferent to the world of literature open and ever opening to them. A man or woman of fifty or sixty makes the best kind of a student. Familiarity with real life and everyday folks gives them an advantage as they read history and general literature. A page of history, biography, literature, travel – holds a great deal more on it for an adult than it can for a youth. Therefore, we urge all people of all ages and social positions to read and think and converse, and never to say or for a moment think "I am too old to study." Nobody is too old to add to his stock of knowledge, nor to find new delight in literature, nor to help keep up interesting home conversation, nor to listen with open ears and eager heart to what thinking men and women are these days thinking and talking about.

*Ever yours,*
*John H. Vincent*
*At Home, 5700 Blackstone Ave.,*
*Chicago, February 18, 1915*

# APPENDIX

*Notes on the Methodism of John Heyl Vincent*

For readers who are not familiar with Methodism, a few brief notes on that tradition's history, polity and terminology may be helpful.[1] Methodism began in England during the early eighteenth century as an evangelical renewal movement within the Church of England. Founders John Wesley (1703-1791) and Charles Wesley (1707-1788) were Anglican priests who were influenced by Puritanism, Pietism, and Arminian theology. They did not plan to start a new denomination. Their intention was for the people who were awakened by Methodist preaching to deepen their faith by participating in weekly class meetings (spiritual growth support group gatherings) and practicing holiness of heart and life as faithful members of the Church of England, where they would receive the sacraments. Eventually Methodists and Anglicans parted ways.

John Heyl Vincent was raised within and served the Methodist Episcopal Church (MEC). The MEC was founded in 1784 as an autonomous American branch of the Methodist movement. The word Episcopal in MEC refers to the fact that American Methodists elected bishops to serve as top administrators in their church

1. This essay attempts to introduce non-Methodists to a few aspects of a complex Christian tradition, focusing on terms and concepts mentioned by Bishop Vincent in his writings. For the sake of brevity, these comments contain numerous simplifications.

hierarchy. It is not a reference to the historically related Episcopal Church.

One of the hallmarks of Wesleyan or Methodist theology is a belief in free will: the concept that individuals can choose to accept God's saving grace or reject it.[1] Because faith was viewed as a personal decision, Methodism was a natural match for the emotional revivalism of the first and second Great Awakenings and the rugged individualism of the sparsely populated American frontier.

Rev. Vincent entered the ministry in the typical fashion for Methodists of his time. His theological education comprised a four-year ministerial apprenticeship while working through a rigorous "course of study" (set of prescribed readings). A college education was not required. Graduate theological education (seminary training) was uncommon among American Methodist clergy until the twentieth century.

Methodist preaching points were on circuits (networks of small churches sharing an elder), stations (a single pastoral charge), or missions (ministry outreach centers). Vincent's pastoral ministry included all three settings.

Church leadership roles in the MEC included class leaders (later, Sunday school teachers and superintendents); local preachers; traveling or "itinerant" clergy of two degrees: deacons preparing for the eldership and fully credentialed elders; presiding elders; and bishops. The system was designed to work something like this: Traveling (itinerant) ministers went from settlement to settlement on a circuit or served a local station. Their duties

1. "On Free Will" is number eight in the Twenty-five Articles of Religion adapted from the Church of England by John Wesley and adopted by the Methodist Episcopal Church during its founding Christmas Conference of 1784.

included preaching, visiting, and presiding over the sacraments.[2] Local preachers held forth on Sundays when itinerant clergy were out on the road. Presiding Elders were charged with overseeing local groups of ministers called districts, holding quarterly conferences (business meetings) in each church of the district, and serving as the bishop's cabinet. Bishops presided over yearly regional clergy meetings called Annual Conferences at which they assigned deacons, elders, and presiding elders to their posts.

In the MEC, local churches did not hire their own pastors. Bishops appointed ministers to serve a year or two at a station, circuit, or mission before being rotated elsewhere within the Annual Conference bounds.[3] Pastors came and went, but class leaders and later Sunday school teachers taught and led discussions weekly, providing a sense of continuity.

Every four years (a quadrennium in Methodist speak), the MEC held a General Conference of representatives from all Annual Conferences to make denomination-wide decisions and to elect new bishops. Clergy could be called to serve on denominational boards and agencies. This is how Vincent moved from the pastoral ministry in Chicago to leading Methodist Sunday School work in New York in 1866.

2. Frontier circuit riders were bearers of Good News, local news, and uplifting reading materials. Under the colportage system, they were expected to sell Methodist publications along their routes.
3. A personal note: Bishop John Wesley Hardt (1921-2017) shared with me that when he was a novice preacher in Texas, it was commonly understood among his colleagues that anyone who was assigned a third year in the same charge was considered too slow a learner to advance far in the ministry. That was the MEC South, not the MEC, but the third-year stigma may have existed in northern Methodism, as well.

Twenty-two years later the MEC General Conference elected Vincent to the episcopacy. His assignments as bishop were based in Buffalo, New York; Topeka, Kansas; and Zurich, Switzerland.[4] The General Conference of 1904 moved Vincent's name to the retired roster over his objections. Late into his life, the bishop emeritus continued to serve on denominational committees.

The nineteenth century was a time of tremendous change for the MEC. The denomination expanded west, establishing Methodist societies and colleges across North America. Organized domestic missionary work began in 1819. International missions followed. Membership grew exponentially, even as disagreements over slavery fractured the church. At the local level, the traditional class meeting system faded and was replaced by prayer meetings and Sunday morning faith formation classes called "Sunday-school."

Throughout the 1800s American Methodists entered the middle class in increasing numbers. Their aspirations for mainstream respectability changed much of the character of church life. The large camp meetings and open emotionalism that spread Methodism like wildfire before the Civil War seemed outdated and uncouth to generations that followed. A more sophisticated church required better-educated clergy.

Not all members of the MEC embraced these changes. Some "old-fashioned" Methodists wanted to rekindle the former fervor. They founded holiness groups that became independent churches and new denominations. As Vincent wrote his autobiography, this defection remained a painful memory.

4. Because Vincent had traveled abroad and because his Sunday School and Chautauqua work were known internationally, he became the first bishop appointed to oversee the work of the MEC annual conferences in Europe.

Although it suffered several divisions, the MEC continued until 1939 when it reunited with the Methodist Protestant Church (established 1828) and the Methodist Episcopal Church, South (established 1845), to form The Methodist Church. Today's United Methodist Church resulted from the 1968 merger of The Methodist Church with the Evangelical United Brethren Church, a kindred Wesleyan Pietist body with German-American roots.

# INDEX

# INDEX

INDEX

# INDEX